QUEST

A World of Change
1900–2000

Bea Stimpson

Stanley Thornes (Publishers) Ltd

First published in 2000 by:
Stanley Thornes (Publishers) Ltd
Delta Place
27 Bath Road
CHELTENHAM GL53 7TH
England

00 01 02 03 04 / 10 9 8 7 6 5 4 3 2 1

A catalogue record for this book is available from the British Library.

ISBN 0-7487-4284-0

Designed and typeset by Clare Park

Edited by Melanie Gray

Illustrated by Francis Bacon, Beverly Curl, Hardlines and Angela Lumley

Cover artwork by Beverly Curl

Picture research by Simon Conti

Printed and bound in Italy by STIGE, Turin

The author wishes to acknowledge Peter Burton, Barry Page and Judi Lavelle of Stanley Thornes for their advice during the preparation of this book.

Thanks are owed to the illustrators for their skill and patience in producing the artwork. She also wishes to thank her teaching colleague, Alan Coulson, for his practical suggestions.

She is particularly indebted to her husband, Michael, for the support he has given.

Acknowledgements

With thanks to the following for permission to reproduce photographs and illustrations:

Bildarchiv Preussischer Kultur Besitz: 102(r)

Bletchley Park: 134

Bundesarchiv, Koblenz: 101, 102(l)

Camera Press: 136, 139, 140

Corbis: 59, 60, 65, 66, 90, 147, 148, 155

Daily Herald: 52

Daily Mirror/Centre for the Study of Cartoon and Caricature: 6

John and Andrew Frost: 10(t)

Hulton Getty: 12, 13, 14(t), 16, 39, 50, 54, 86(t), 89(t), 106, 107(b), 114, 115, 117, 118

Illustrated London News: 9(both), 10(b), 14(b), 19(t), 146(l)

Imperial War Museum, London: 24, 25, 26, 30, 31, 32, 35, 36, 37, 41, 44, 45, 94, 104, 113, 116, 119, 143

David King Collection: 69, 72, 73, 74, 75(both), 76, 80, 83, 84(both), 85(all), 123

Magnum Photos/Raymond Depardon: 124

Mary Evans Picture Library: 5, 11, 17, 18, 19(b), 20(t), 21, 23, 38, 49, 88, 89(b), 91, 98, 99, 103(l)

Mary Evans Picture Library/Alexander Meledin Collection: 122, 128

Barry Page: 48

Peter Newark's Pictures: 46, 137, 144, 146(r)

Public Record Office: 8, 133(both)

Punch Cartoon Library: 20(b)

Rex Features: 157

RIA-Novosti, London: 132

Sainsbury's Supermarkets Ltd: 7

Philip Sauvain: 34, 42, 107(t)

Suddeutscher Verlag Bilderdienst: 93, 95

theartarchive: 43, 103(r)

Topham Picturepoint: 58, 61, 100, 109, 138

TRH Pictures: 127

Ullstein Bilderdienst: 86(b), 92, 96(both), 131

Wiener Library, London: 97, 110

Every effort has been made to contact copyright holders we apologise if any have been inadvertently overlooked.

Contents

1 A new era   **5**

From Victorians to Edwardians   5

Alliances and agreements   6

2 Science and technology   **7**

Mass society   7

Mass entertainment   8

Mass communication   9

Mass titbits   10

A substitute horse   11

Mass commuting   12

Mass production   13

A flying start   14

The new physics   15

Madame Marie Curie   16

3 The Suffragettes   **17**

The role of women   17

Suffragists   18

Suffragettes   19

'Cats and mice'   20

4 Background to the First World War   **21**

The causes of the War   21

Assassination at Sarajevo   22

Escalation to war   23

5 The two sides   **24**

Patriotism   24

The British Expeditionary Force   25

The Imperial German Army   26

6 Early campaigns   **27**

Schlieffen and stalemate   27

The First World War   28

Other campaigns   29

7 The Home Front   **30**

The Home Front   30

The propaganda campaign   31

Women at war   32

8 War at sea and in the air   **33**

The war at sea   33

Aeroplane warfare   34

9 Trench warfare and the Western Front   **35**

The Western Front   35

Trench life   36

No man's land   37

New weapons: gas and flame-throwers   38

New weapon: the tank   39

The Front Line, 1914–1917   40

The Somme   41

U-boats and the USA   42

Passchendaele   43

One letter, Passchendaele   44

One death, Passchendaele   45

10 The end of the First World War   **46**

The 1918 German offensive   46

'Backs to the wall'   47

Dignity in death   48

11 Peace-making and peace-keeping   **49**

Democracy in Britain   49

The 'Big Three'   50

The Treaty of Versailles   51

German reaction to the Treaty   52

Other peace treaties   53

The League of Nations   54

The League in the 1920s   55

12 The USA, 1918–1939   **56**

The USA   56

Economic boom   57

The Roaring Twenties   58

Prohibition and crime   59

The 'melting pot'   60

Poverty amidst plenty   61

13 Boom then crash   **62**

The Wall Street Crash   62

The Great Depression   63

14 President Roosevelt and the New Deal   **64**

The first one hundred days   64

'Action and action now'   65

The first New Deal   66

The second New Deal   67

15 Tsarist rule in Russia   **68**

The Russian Empire   68

Tsar Nicholas II   69

Opposition to the Tsar   70

Marxist communism   71

The Revolution of 1905   72

Russia at war   73

16 The Russian Revolution   **74**

The February Revolution, 1917   74

All power to the Bolsheviks   75

The October Revolution, 1917   76

17 Lenin in power   **77**

Lenin in power   77

Civil war, 1918–1921   78

War communism and the new economic policy   79

Contents

18 Stalin in power — 80

Stalin in power — 80

Collectivisation and dekulakisation — 81

The five-year plans — 82

Stalin's purges — 83

Totalitarianism — 84

Communist dictatorship — 85

19 Italy — 86

Fascism — 86

Dictatorships — 87

Towards totalitarianism — 88

Fascist dictatorship in Italy — 89

20 Germany — 90

Adolf Hitler — 90

The Munich Putsch — 91

The time of struggle — 92

The rise of the Nazis — 93

From Chancellor to Dictator — 94

The Night of the Long Knives — 95

Minorities and Jews — 96

Kristallnacht — 97

Education in Germany — 98

Hitler Youth — 99

Adulthood in Nazi Germany — 100

'Bread and work' — 101

Totalitarianism — 102

Fascist dictatorship in Germany — 103

21 The road to war — 104

Rearmament — 104

The League of Nations — 105

Austria — 106

Sudetenland and the Munich Conference — 107

The end of appeasement — 108

22 War in Europe — 109

Evacuation — 109

Poland — 110

Norway and Denmark — 111

Luxembourg, Holland and Belgium — 112

Dunkirk and the fall of France — 113

23 War in Britain — 114

The battle for Britain — 114

Luftwaffe versus RAF — 115

The Battle of Britain — 116

The Blitz — 117

Women at war — 118

The Home Guard — 119

24 The widening war — 120

Mussolini enters the war — 120

Operation Barbarossa — 121

War in Russia — 122

Into the space and snow — 123

Into the night and fog — 124

Pearl Harbor — 125

World war — 126

25 Major turning points — 127

Japanese successes halted — 127

Stalingrad — 128

El Alamein — 129

From defensive to offensive — 130

The Final Solution — 131

26 The secret war — 132

Resistance — 132

The SOE — 133

Ultra, Enigma and Colossus — 134

27 Blockade and bombs — 135

The Battle of the Atlantic — 135

'Happy times' again — 136

Mass bombing — 137

28 The end of the Third Reich — 138

Overlord and D-Day — 138

From Normandy to the Rhine — 139

Secret weapons — 140

Germany threatened — 141

Victory in Europe — 142

Kingdom of the Night — 143

29 The end of the Second World War — 144

Bushido and kamikaze — 144

No surrender — 145

The end of the Second World War — 146

30 Towards Cold War — 147

The United Nations — 147

Towards Cold War — 148

The Iron Curtain — 149

31 The Cold War — 150

Key events — 150

The arms race: nuclear weapons — 151

The Berlin Blockade — 152

The Berlin Wall — 153

The Cuban Missile Crisis — 154

Nuclear war? — 155

Back from the abyss — 156

The collapse of communism — 157

32 Kings and queens of Great Britain and Ireland — 158

Index — 159

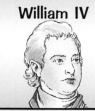
From Victorians to Edwardians

Queen Victoria died on January 22, 1901 after a reign of 64 years. Through her marriage to Albert, and the marriages of her children, the royal family was connected with rulers of countries such as Russia, Germany, Spain, Romania, Norway and Sweden.

The status of Britain among the world powers was reflected in the fact that five sovereigns, nine crown princes or heirs apparent, and 40 other princes and grand dukes attended her funeral. Britain's Empire, the largest in the world, covered both hemispheres and was known as 'the Empire on which the sun never sets'. Her navy, the most powerful in the world, still 'ruled the waves'. Victoria's titles now passed to her son, Edward VII, King of Great Britain and Ireland and Emperor of India. One mourner at Victoria's funeral was her grandson, the Kaiser of Germany, Wilhelm II.

Germany, as a nation-state, had been formed only in 1870 and was the strongest military power on the continent. The Germans wanted to gain more overseas empire so that they too could have a 'place in the sun' as Britain had. Before his return to Germany, the Kaiser let it be known that he favoured an alliance between the two nations in which Britain would keep the seas and Germany would be responsible for the land. With such an alliance, he said, 'not a mouse would stir in Europe without our permission'.

▲ King Edward VII, the first king of the House of Saxe-Coburg Gotha

German states unite into one Empire	Dual Alliance: Germany and Austria-Hungary	Becomes Triple Alliance with addition of Italy	versus	Dual Alliance: France and Russia	Entente Cordiale: Britain and France	Friendly agreement between Britain and Russia	Britain now in Triple Entente (but not legally bound)
1871	1879	1882		1893	1904	1907	

Alliances and agreements

Did Britain welcome the idea of an alliance with Germany?

Not particularly. She knew that Germany had already formed a Triple Alliance with Austria-Hungary and Italy and did not want to help defend their borders against Russia.

She was also wary of Germany's plans to build up her navy as Germany had begun the construction of a High Seas Fleet in 1897. The Kaiser wanted to complete the reorganisation of his navy so that 'it shall be in a position internationally to win for Germany that place we have yet to achieve'.

On a personal level, King Edward VII thoroughly disliked his nephew, though in public this was never expressed.

How emperor-kings conducted themselves in public and what they said was noted and considered important in international relations. Edward took his royal duties seriously and undertook a series of goodwill visits abroad. These included a very successful trip to Paris in 1903. Speaking excellent French and using his charm and diplomacy, he helped to win over the French and paved the way for a new Entente Cordiale, a friendly agreement in 1904.

▲ A British cartoon from 1905 of the Entente Cordiale, with British warships in the background

In 1907 another friendly agreement – this time with Russia, which already had an alliance with France – meant that Britain became part of a Triple Entente. Though in no way legally committed to France and Russia, Britain had to make it clear where her obligations would lie if ever there was a war in Europe.

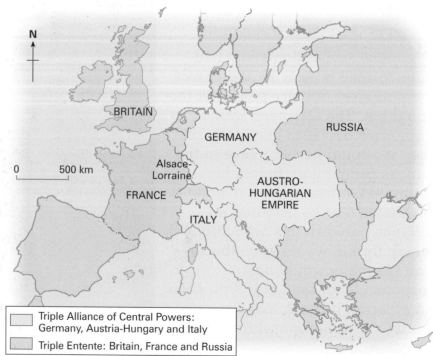

► The Triple Alliance and the Triple Entente

Triple Alliance of Central Powers: Germany, Austria-Hungary and Italy

Triple Entente: Britain, France and Russia

Mass society

Edward VII was a popular monarch. He brought back pomp, ceremony and gaiety to a court which, under the widowed Victoria, had been drab and solemn for too long. The King managed to combine his more serious royal duties at home and abroad with an inexhaustible pursuit of pleasure. He enjoyed horse racing, shooting parties, yachting, banquets and, above all, the company of beautiful women, regardless of social origin. In Edwardian Britain, social distinctions were usually clear-cut. The gulfs and contrasts between the upper, middle and lower classes remained unchanged and marked, yet the world in which the Edwardians lived was changing dramatically. The technological changes ushered in by the continuing industrial revolution had created a 'mass society'.

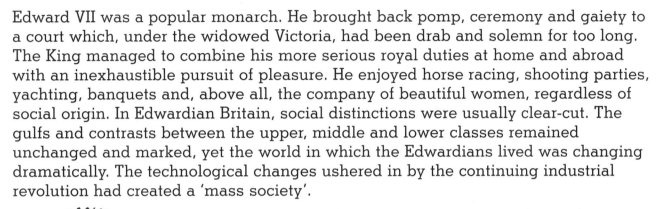

What does that mean?

Early inventions and innovations had been adopted and improved by increasingly industrialised countries such as the USA, France and Germany, as well as Britain.

People in these countries began to enjoy the use of the developments of these inventions. They shared the same means of mass communications such as the telephone. They shared the use of mass transport such as the bicycle. Commodities such as tea and bacon reached mass markets. Food could now be frozen, canned and shipped worldwide. Chain stores and department stores, some American-owned, were set up in Britain for people to purchase these mass commodities. The 'mass society' created new jobs. Wealthy and successful businessmen were starting to be accepted into the upper classes.

▲ Catering for a mass market: shop assistants in the meat department of J. Sainsbury, a new chain store of the period

7

Mass entertainment

Shop assistants would often be expected to work from 7.30am to 9.15pm, and for the majority of employees the working days were just as long. However, from 1870 four bank holidays had been introduced, and a Saturday half-day holiday was customary by 1900.

How did the Edwardians spend their leisure time?

GREAT WESTERN RAILWAY.

HUNTING SEASON

HUNTING SEASON TICKETS.

GROOMS. REDUCED FARES

HORSES. REDUCED RATES.

FULL PARTICULARS AT THE STATIONS AND OFFICES OF THE COMPANY.

PADDINGTON STATION.   JAMES C. INGLIS, General Manager.

▲ Hunting remained an upper-class sport

Sport, and the gambling that often accompanied it, was enjoyed by all classes.

The King's horses won the Derby three times, and horse-racing, prize-fighting, rugby, tennis, golf, cricket and football were particularly popular.

Football was now a professional sport. The amateur teams set up by organisations such as church and chapel groups and by work places had been formed into a Football League in 1888. The original twelve league clubs came from industrial areas: six from the Midlands and six from Lancashire. Sport rapidly became, with electrical amplification and flood-lighting, a mass spectacle. The working man could measure out his life in terms not of a *country* calendar but of a *sporting* one.

Towns offered public houses, working-men's clubs, gentlemen's clubs, restaurants, theatres and music-halls. However, it was the invention of the cinematograph that created a new form of mass entertainment to rival the music-hall. In December 1895 an incredulous French crowd watched 'moving' film of scenes – such as a train leaving a station – made by the Lumière brothers, Louis and Auguste. By 1909 over 20 million people a week in the USA were attending the nickelodeon, a showroom for the projection of films. The first purpose-built cinema in Britain was opened in Colne, Lancashire in 1908. By 1914 there were 400 cinemas in London alone.

dle telegraph nted by Charles eatstone and am Cooke	Cable laid across Channel: London and Paris linked	Transatlantic cable installed	Invention of telephone by Alexander Graham Bell	1 in 50 people in USA had a telephone	Wireless telegraphy: Cornwall to Newfoundland
7	1851	1866	1875	1900	1901

Mass communication

Were films silent at that time?

Yes, although means of transmitting speech was possible by then via the telephone, which had been invented in 1875.

Even before its invention, scientists had begun to investigate ways of transmitting sound without wires. It was Guglielmo Marconi, an Italian-British engineer and physicist based in Britain, who developed the wireless means of transmitting messages. He began by introducing large directional aerials for both transmitters and receivers. He mastered the technique of 'tuning' both devices to the same wavelength. In 1895 he transmitted beyond the line of sight, with a hill between the transmitter and the receiver. In 1901, on an aerial supported by a kite, Marconi (waiting in St John's, Newfoundland) received a morse message from Cornwall, England. Radiation (radio) had spanned the Atlantic.

The British government made use of the radio for their navy. In 1903 the headquarters of the British First Army Corps made successful contact by wireless telegraphy with ships of Channel Squadron. This form of communication was to provide the means for messages from ship to ship and from naval headquarters to ships at sea. The Germans fitted radios into their Zeppelin airships. All nations began to create codes and ciphers to ensure security.

▲ Employment for women in a telephone exchange

▲ Guglielmo Marconi

A dramatic civilian use of radio was demonstrated in 1910. A morse code telegraph message was sent to the captain of the *Montrose*, a liner sailing in Canadian waters off Quebec, warning him that a suspected murderer, Dr Crippen, and his mistress were on board. Crippen was arrested on arrival in Canada and later convicted. In 1912, when the British liner *Titanic* sank in the Atlantic Ocean after hitting an iceberg, a wireless distress signal brought vessels to the scene.

| New York Journal | Daily Mail | Daily Express | Daily Sketch | Daily Mirror | La Petit Journal, France | La Tribuna, Italy | Japan had popula mass-circulation newspapers |

Popular press

Mass titbits

The Crippen case and the *Titanic* disaster were quickly reported in the popular press of the day. Advances in wire and wireless communications meant news-gathering was now a matter of minutes not months.

Technology had transformed the newspaper industry. Compositors used keyboards. From 1902 rotary presses could print 72,000 copies an hour, and printing was possible on both sides of a continuous roll of wood-pulp paper.

> When did the mass circulation of newspapers start?

> When the mass of the population could read, and wanted to read what was available!

The introduction of state elementary education for boys and girls from 1870 led to an increasingly literate workforce in Britain. It was George Newnes who first created a large readership through the publication of his weekly magazine, *Titbits*. By offering titbits (interesting snippets of news), sales totalled 900,000 copies within three months. One of his contributors, Alfred Harmsworth, tried a similar formula in his halfpenny paper, the *Daily Mail*. All news stories and articles were kept short. It had paragraphs of gossip about prominent men and women. Parliamentary and company reports were cut to short summaries of what was sensational or informative. Sports were well covered and included a column of racing tips. Women had two columns devoted to fashion and home matters. Advertisements, which provided most of the profits, were a feature. This titbit presentation was so successful that similar newspapers followed. All these papers reinforced the patriotism that was popular at the time. The *Daily Express*, in its first editorial, asserted, 'our policy is patriotic; our policy is the British Empire'.

STOP PRESS

CRIPPEN ARRESTED.

DRAMATIC SCENE ABOARD THE MONTROSE.

FUGITIVES TAKEN INTO CUSTODY AT END OF VOYAGE.

Father Point (Rimouski), July 31.— Crippen and Le Neve have both been identified and arrested.—Reuter.

INSPECTOR DEW BOARDS LINER

Father Point, July 31.

By special arrangement Inspector Dew this morning boarded the steamer Montrose from a rowing boat leaving the numerous newspaper correspondents to follow in the Government tender Eureka.

The object of this proceeding was to enable the detective to make the arrest without perviously arousing the suspicions of "Dr." Crippen and Miss Le Neve.—Reuter.

Mr. Dew was disguised as a pilot.—Central News.

▲ The *News of the World* 'scoops' the Crippen story, July 31, 1910

TRY IT IN YOUR BATH.

SCRUBB'S.

A MARVELLOUS PREPARATION.

Refreshing as a Turkish Bath.
Invaluable for Toilet Purposes.
Splendid Cleansing Preparation for the Hair.
Removes Stains and Grease Spots from Clothing.
Allays the Irritation caused by Mosquito Bites.
Invigorating in Hot Climates.
Restores the Colour to Carpets.
Cleans Plate and Jewellery.
Softens Hard Water.
So Vivifying after Cricket, Motoring and other Sports.

"MAKES HOME, SWEET HOME IN DEED."

▲ A typical newspaper advertisement of the time

A substitute horse

The British had invented the external combustion engine powered by steam, which gave rise to the railway locomotive and powered ships. The French, German and Americans pioneered the *internal* combustion engine, where heat is produced inside rather than outside the cylinder.

This engine, powered first by coal-gas and then by petrol, gave rise to the motor car and the aeroplane.

A French engineer, Etienne Lenoir, first produced a gas engine where a mixture of coal-gas and air was sucked into a cylinder and ignited by an electric spark. The force of expansion following ignition pushed a piston, which in turn rotated a wheel. In 1876 a German engineer, Nikolaus Otto, improved Lenoir's engine by producing a four-stroke combustion engine in which ignition took place at every stroke.

What were the advantages of gas over steam power?

The engine was smaller. Its fuel consumption was less. It needed no preliminary heating up. It developed more power in relation to its weight.

The drawback of gas was that it could be used only in stationary vehicles. In 1884 Karl Benz adapted a gas engine to burn liquid fuel by means of a carburettor and fitted it to a tricycle. Gottlieb Daimler had discovered that petrol was superior to gas and he made the first petrol-driven four-wheeled car in 1887. This was basically a horse-drawn carriage with shafts and horse removed! Petrol was the substitute horse and petrol energy was rated in terms of 'horse power'.

▲ Petrol and trap rather than pony and trap

11

Bicycles manufactured in Britain	Modern 'safety bicycle'	Pneumatic tyre	Electric railway	Electric tramway	Motor taxi-cab	Motor bus	Last horse-drawn bus in London
1869	1880s	1888	1900	1901	1903	1905	1911

Mass commuting

The car was at this time an 'expensive toy' for the wealthy, so it was the bicycle that first enjoyed widespread popularity. The modern 'safety' bicycle, with wheels almost equal in size and with a rear-wheel chain-drive, was produced in the 1880s. Cycling became comfortable as well as safe when, in 1888, John Boyd Dunlop, from Belfast, produced a pneumatic tyre with a separate air-filled inner tube. The inventions that helped to develop the bicycle – the steel spokes, roller bearings and, above all, the pneumatic tyre – later helped the development of motoring. Cycles, therefore, did not remain in the fast lane for long.

By 1903 the number of cars on British roads was approaching 20,000. Licences were required by law for all motorists and the speed limit was raised to 32kph. Reckless drivers on country roads were caught in 'speed traps' and fined. In towns the public now had the choice of several means of transport. From 1903 motor taxi-cabs were available for hire. There were electric tramways, electric railways and, in London from 1905, the electric Underground (the 'tube'). In that same year the London Omnibus Company, the largest owner of horse-drawn buses, decided to change to motor buses. On October 25, 1911, London's only remaining horse-drawn bus left London Bridge on its last journey.

The tram, bus and tube carried more and more people out to the ever-expanding suburbs. The age of mass commuting had arrived.

▲ Motor buses in Piccadilly in about 1910

Mass production

'I will build a motor car for the great multitude...'

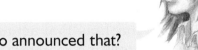

Who announced that?

Henry Ford in 1907, when he was about to set up a production line for his Model T in Detroit, USA.

In order to build a vehicle cheap enough for the masses to afford, he developed techniques for mass production. Work was carried mechanically by conveyor belt at waist height to the factory workers. Manufacture was divided up into the smallest possible unit operations, and each operation was performed by a different worker.

Ford appreciated that the work was monotonous, so, to compensate, in 1914 he guaranteed a minimum wage of $5 a day – more than double the rate then being paid. His innovation worked. The 'Tin Lizzies', made of good-quality materials, rolled off the assembly-lines for worldwide distribution, reaching 1 million by 1915. As production and sales went up, prices came down. Ford's first British factory opened in Manchester in 1911. The first Briton to use Ford's mass production methods was William Morris of Oxford.

Was the military significance of this invention realised early on?

Yes, although military use of the petrol engine concentrated on four-wheeled armoured cars, rather than 'tracked' vehicles that spread their weight over the ground.

In 1906 a German firm used a lorry chassis on which to mount a high-angle 50mm anti-aircraft gun in a turret. In 1910 another German firm, Krupps, produced a much more sophisticated 75mm model. These machines were not just for counter-attack against airships. They were also aimed at a new sort of flying machine: the aeroplane.

▲ An early German anti-aircraft gun

13

First man-carrying powered flight: Wright brothers (American)	First cross-Channel flight: Blériot (French)	London to Manchester air race won by Paulhan	Loop the loop and upside down: Pégoud (French)	Planes reach 138kph carry no more than people; stay in air fo up to 4 hours
1903 December 17	1909 July 13	1910	1913	1914

A *flying start*

Two bicycle mechanics from the USA, the brothers Wilbur and Orville Wright, made the first flying machine that actually worked. After spending many years experimenting with man-carrying gliders, they then decided to fix propellers to a glider, using power from an internal combustion (petrol) engine to revolve them.

On December 17, 1903, near Kitty Hawk in North Carolina, Orville piloted a bi-plane with two propellers driven by a 12-horse-power engine. This first man-carrying powered flight lasted twelve seconds, flew a distance of 37 metres and rose to a height of just three metres.

▲ The first flight in a heavier-than-air machine

By 1905 the brothers had made nearly 300 flights, some lasting nearly twenty minutes and reaching a distance of 36km. By this time their aeroplanes could fly a circular course and perform aerial manoeuvres such as banking and 'figure of eight'.

The brothers failed to receive recognition in America, so, in 1908, Wilbur went to France where engineers gave him every encouragement. Development was rapid, and it was a Frenchman, Louis Blériot, who, in 1909, flew over the English Channel in a 25-horse-powered monoplane. In 1913 another Frenchman, Aldolphe Pégoud, was the first man to fly 'loop the loop' and upside down.

▲ A safe landing behind Dover Castle for Blériot, about 43 minutes after leaving Calais

Was the military significance of this invention realised?

The French and British governments both became interested.

In 1908 the French army ordered 50 Wright aeroplanes and experimented with petrol bombs and bombs containing inflammable liquid. The British government at first failed to recognise the aeroplane's military potential, but, by 1909, the Wrights were advising the government about this new aerial science.

ory of Relativity: k on relating mass energy laid theory nuclear physics	Quantum Theory: radiation not transferred in continuous stream but in 'quanta'	Discovered that the atom could be split	Discovered that atomic model atoms each had nucleus with electrons orbiting around it
tein	Planck	Rutherford	Bohr

The new physics

Another science which got off to a flying start in the early 20th century was nuclear science. Startling discoveries overturned the laws contained in the 'old' physics stemming from Isaac Newton's theory developed in the 18th century. Newton suggested that all matter was composed of solid, unsplittable atoms. He thought that there was 'no ordinary power being able to divide what God himself made one in the first creation'.

It was the discovery of radioactivity (radiation) that led to this theory being challenged. In 1896 a French physicist, Henri Becquerel, discovered that the element uranium radiated powerful invisible rays. Ernest Rutherford, a British physicist, found two sets of rays emanating from uranium, and called them 'alpha' and 'beta'. Simultaneously a French physicist, Pierre Curie, found two sets of rays emanating from radium – a new element that was much more radioactive than uranium. Radium had been discovered by Pierre's wife, Marie, a Polish chemist, and it was she who suggested that radioactivity was caused not by something acting on the substance from outside it, but by agitating particles inside the atom.

In 1911, using radium samples, Rutherford discovered that the alpha rays were actually particles from within individual atoms shooting out as they disintegrated. Furthermore, these alpha particles could smash other atoms. This new physics led to a new model of the atom: an atom that was mostly empty inside but with a central core – the nucleus. In 1905 a German physicist, Albert Einstein, suggested that there was almost unbelievable power locked up inside each atom. The quest turned to unlocking that power.

▲ A modern atom, with electrons orbiting around the nucleus

Birth of Marie Sklodowska, Warsaw	Moves to Paris	Marries Pierre Curie	Isolates polonium and radium	Curies awarded Nobel Prize jointly with Becquerel	Marie Curie awarded Nobel Prize	Dies of radiation poisoning	Daughter Irene and her husband Frederic Joliet win Nobel Prize for discovery of artificial radioactivity
1867	1891	1895	1898	1903	1911	1934 July 4	1935

Madame Marie Curie

How did Marie Curie discover radium?

She observed that the radioactivity of pitchblende, a rich uranium ore, was four times as large as it should be if it contained only uranium.

▲ Marie and Pierre Curie

By 1898, with the help of Pierre, she had extracted two unknown elements, polonium and radium, from pitchblende. They then had to convince the doubting scientific world of the powerful radioactivity of radium. Working in a laboratory no better than a shed, the Curies first had to sift tonnes of pitchblende. It then had to be ground down, boiled with soda, separated into a solid material and a liquid, the solid being dissolved with acid. Endless processes then followed – mixing, dissolving, heating, distilling, filtering and crystallising. After four years, a tenth of a gramme of pure, pale-blue phosphorescent radium was revealed to the world.

In 1903 the Curies, jointly with Becquerel, were awarded the Nobel Prize for physics. In 1911 Marie was awarded a second Nobel Prize, this time for chemistry.

By this time, it had been found that radium could destroy diseased cells and so was used in cancer therapy. Her work measured the purity and strength of radium preparations and was invaluable knowledge for therapists preparing doses for treatment. What was not known was that radioactive substances could make air radioactive and cause radiation sickness which permanently damaged the body.

Marie herself, after working for 25 years without protection, died of this incurable illness. Her work had helped to save and prolong the lives of millions of people. She had opened up a new science – nuclear physics – and, as the first female Doctor of Science in Europe, led the way for women in a profession previously dominated by men.

t public school girls: North don Collegiate	Forster's Education Act	Married Women's Property Act allowed women to keep earnings	Law allowed women to attend university	Married Women's Property Act allowed women to own property	Women allowed entry to Royal College of Surgeons
0	1870	1870	1875	1882	1895

THE SUFFRAGETTES
3

The role of women

Madame Curie had proved that women could be the intellectual equals of men – and pioneers as well. In 1891 she had had to leave Poland for Paris to continue her studies because Polish women were not allowed to attend university at that time. In Britain a law of 1875 did allow women to attend university. Colleges for 'young ladies', the beginnings of public schools for girls in 1850 and, in 1870, the start of state education for girls as well as boys, led to important social changes.

Women began to train as doctors, surgeons and lawyers. Teaching and nursing became popular careers, though teachers – like female civil servants – had to resign if they married.

Working-class women had little choice. Many worked long hours in factories, laundries or in trades such as dressmaking. Others found work in 'new' jobs such as those of shop assistant, telephonist and typist. The largest single form of female employment, however, remained domestic service, which reached a peak of $1\frac{1}{2}$ million in 1913.

As working-class women cleaned the hearth, middle-class women, once they were married, were expected to become 'angels of the hearth'. Most married women of all classes, though, spent their 20s and 30s pregnant and looking after their families.

▲ Young ladies at the bench: the science laboratory at the University of Leeds, founded in 1904

Did women own their own houses?

Not until 1882 were married women allowed to own property and dispose of it as they wished. Thus, in the early 20th century, only a few women were householders.

All laws concerning women's issues – such as contraception, divorce and equal pay – were still made by an all-male parliament. As women slowly became more independent, the demand for emancipation (freedom) from masculine control grew.

Reform Act: 7% of men could vote in general elections	Men and women could vote for Poor Law Guardians	Reform Act: 16% of men could vote	Women could vote for and stand for election to school boards	Reform Act: 28½% of men could vote	Women cou vote in local elections
1832	1834	1867	1870	1884	1886

Suffragists

Who were the Suffragists?

Suffrage means the right to vote. Suffragist was the name given to women who joined a suffrage society to campaign to be given the vote on the same basis as men.

Campaigning for votes for women was not new, nor was it dismissed by all male MPs. As early as 1867, the MP and notable philosopher, John Stuart Mill, had introduced a bill for women's suffrage in the House of Commons. Though defeated, similar bills were introduced nearly every year after that.

An early leader of the suffrage movement, Lydia Becker, had formed a Suffrage Committee in Manchester to collect signatures for Mill's petition, and further committees in other towns helped to keep up the pressure on parliament. In 1897 Millicent Fawcett, a sister of the first registered female doctor in England, Elizabeth Garret Anderson, united over 500 local suffrage groups into the National Union of Women's Suffrage Societies (NUWSS). The group's tactics remained peaceful and legal: petitions, meetings, pamphlets and letters to politicians were the methods used.

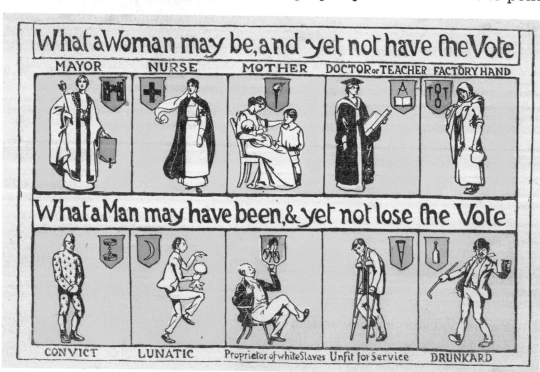

▲ A postcard of 1912 produced by the Suffrage Atelier, a group of women artists who designed publicity material

In 1903, however, Emmeline Pankhurst, a member of the Manchester suffrage group, became impatient at the lack of progress made and decided on a change of tactics. With her daughters, Christabel and Sylvia, Mrs Pankhurst formed the breakaway Women's Social and Political Union (WSPU). In 1905 it transferred its headquarters to London. Its object was immediate enfranchisement by political action. In January 1906, after reporting on various incidents, the *Daily Mail* christened these new types of campaigners 'Suffragettes', and the name stuck.

'Put me on an island where the girls are few,
Put me with the most ferocious lions in the zoo,
Put me on a treadmill, and I'll never never fret,
But for pity's sake don't put me with a Suffragette.'

music-hall song

Suffragettes

What was the difference between the Suffragists and Suffragettes?

In one word, militancy. Militant means 'engaged in warfare'.

The WSPU decided that argument and persuasion were not enough. Its members deliberately broke the law to draw attention to their cause. They also lobbied politicians, particularly those in the Liberal Party, which won the general election of 1906.

Hundreds of Liberal MPs did favour votes for women, and the Prime Minister, Campbell-Bannerman, encouraged the Suffragettes to 'go on pestering'. This they certainly did. They wrote slogans on walls. They had themselves delivered as human parcels to Downing Street. They burnt words in acid on the putting greens on Birmingham Golf Course. They changed the King's white marker flags on his private golf course at Balmoral for purple, green and white ones, the colours of the WSPU. They lowered themselves through skylights during political meetings. They fought with police when they were refused entry to Westminster. They chained themselves to railings so that they could not be taken away easily. This form of protest happened so often that *Punch* magazine published a fake advertisement:

▲ Suffragettes chaining themselves to the railings in Downing Street, 1908

Chains! Chains! Chains!
Very strong with automatic police-proof padlocks and railing attachment complete. State waist measurement.

How did the authorities respond to these activities?

They sent hundreds of Suffragettes to prison.

Once there, some women began to refuse food and were released when they became ill. To prevent others from avoiding their sentence, the government decided to have them forcibly fed – an unpleasant and painful procedure, in which liquid food is pumped into the stomach via the mouth or nostrils.

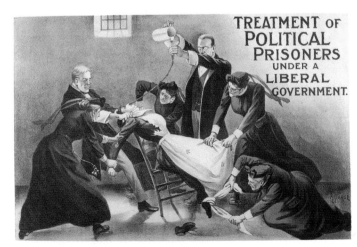

▲ A Suffragette propaganda poster showing the harshness of force-feeding

'Cats and mice'

▲ A Suffragette propaganda poster

In 1913 the government halted the unpopular procedure of force-feeding and instead brought in a Prisoners' (Temporary Discharge) Bill. Starving women were released and rearrested as soon as they had recovered. This became known as the 'Cat and Mouse Act' because, after freedom of usually a week, the police 'pounced' to catch the Suffragette mice over again.

By this time, after Liberal promises, as well as debates and votes in parliament, had produced no results, the Suffragettes intensified their campaign. In March 1912, using toffee hammers, they smashed hundreds of panes of glass in department stores in London. Days later more shops were attacked. Further attacks on property included the use of fire and homemade bombs.

The incident that produced the most publicity was the death of Emily Wilding Dickenson, who threw herself in front of the King's horse during the Derby and died of head wounds two days later.

Did these actions win more support for the Suffragettes?

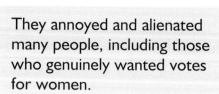

They annoyed and alienated many people, including those who genuinely wanted votes for women.

▲ The new independent woman at her own hearth: 'Militant Suffragist (after long and futile efforts to light a fire for her tea-kettle). "And to think that only yesterday I burnt two pavilions and a church!"' A cartoon from *Punch* magazine.

Others regarded the Suffragettes as irresponsible and unfit to vote, especially the Anti-Suffrage movements of men and women. They thought that women were meant to be 'ladylike' and enjoy looking in shop windows, not smashing them! One supportive MP, Winston Churchill, remarked, 'I have to say, I think your cause has marched backwards'. Courageous and sincere, the Suffragettes pushed forward relentlessly.

The causes of the War

Why did Britain go to war with Germany?

Tensions between the countries of the Triple Entente and the Triple Alliance had been growing during the Edwardian era.

Britain, for example, with the largest empire in the world, kept the largest navy to protect it. She could not understand why the Kaiser, with such a small empire, needed to build up *his* navy.

Alarmed at this, and to help maintain superiority at sea, in 1906 Britain began to build a new type of battleship: Dreadnoughts. Germany responded by producing her own new ships and began to build more than Britain. To emphasise that the balance of power lay firmly with her, Britain made sure that from 1910 she outproduced Germany.

The arms race at sea was echoed on land. All the Great Powers, except Britain, introduced conscription (compulsory military service) and expanded their armies. They argued that large armies ensured peace as they discouraged invasion from other countries. Germany's army, meanwhile, became recognised as the most powerful in the world.

▲ The formidable British fleet

The Kaiser persisted in his ambition to find a 'place in the sun'. In 1905, on visiting the French colony of Morocco, he made a speech supporting the Moroccans in their struggle against France. The French were furious and it took an international conference to settle the dispute. Britain supported France and a humiliated Germany backed down.

Morocco was again the scene of a dispute when, in 1911, the Kaiser sent a gunboat to Agadir, a port there. Britain and France, suspecting that the Kaiser intended to build a naval base at Agadir, protested. Again, the Kaiser withdrew. But, as Britain supported France, so Germany backed Austria in another tension-causing incident.

Assassination at Sarajevo

In 1908 Austria took over the provinces of Bosnia and Herzegovina in an unstable part of Europe, the Balkans. Serbia and her close ally Russia protested, but, as Austria was backed by her ally Germany, neither took action.

In 1912 and 1913, during a series of local wars which pushed Turkey out of Europe, Serbia emerged as the strongest country in the Balkans. Austria, fearing Serbia's and Russia's growing military strength, looked for an excuse to crush Serbia.

Many Serbs who lived in the Austrian-ruled Bosnia wanted *their* areas to be joined to Serbia. Some, including members of a group called the Black Hand, were prepared to use violence to achieve this end. On Sunday June 28, 1914, the heir to the throne of Austria, the Archduke Franz Ferdinand, accompanied by his wife Sophia, undertook an official visit to Sarajevo, the capital of Bosnia. Six Bosnian-Serbs, members of the Black Hand and armed with pistols and bombs, merged with the crowd waiting to welcome the Duke.

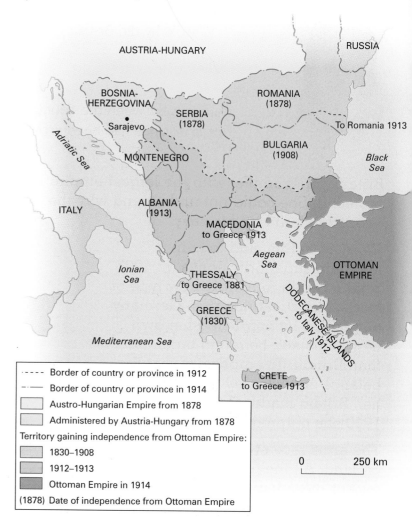

▲ A map of the Balkan Wars, 1912–1913

As the motor cavalcade drove down the main street, one member threw a bomb. It missed the Duke's car but injured an officer in the following car. Later that day the Duke decided to visit the officer in hospital. The driver, not informed of the change of plan, rejoined the original route. Reversing to join the new route, the car halted in front of another of the would-be assassins, Gavrilo Princip. Seizing his chance, Princip shot the Archduke and his wife, who both died soon afterwards. Austria now had the excuse they needed to crush Serbia.

many declares on Russia	Germany moves army towards France and Belgium	French army on war footing	Germany invades Belgium and declares war on France	Britain orders Germany to withdraw from Belgium	Britain enters war against Germany	Austria declares war on Russia
4 August 1	August 2	August 3	August 4	Midnight	August 6	

Escalation to war

Although there was no available evidence to prove that the assassins were acting on behalf of the Serbian government, this did not deter the Austrians from taking action.

After checking that they had the full support of Germany, they decided to send an ultimatum to Serbia. The calendar of events is as follows:

July 23		Austria delivers ten-point ultimatum to Serbia and gives them two days to accept.
July 25	am	Tsar of Russia announces support for Serbia. Places troops at a 'period preparatory to war'.
	pm	Bolstered by Russia's support, Serbia accepts all but one of Austria's demands – that Austrian officials should be involved in the investigation of all those involved in the assassination.
July 28		Austria rejects this reply and declares war on Serbia.
July 29		As Austria and Serbia mobilise, Russia, with the support of France, announces partial mobilisation. Diplomats from the Great Powers work feverishly to contain the dispute.
July 31		Russia moves to general mobilisation. Germany sends ultimatum to Russia and France, warning of general mobilisation unless Russia suspends war measures.
August 1		France orders mobilisation. Germany declares war on Russia.
August 2		Germany delivers ultimatum to Belgium, demanding use of territory in operations against France. Belgium, as a neutral country, refuses.
August 3		German troops enter Belgium. Germany declares war on France.
August 4		Britain sends a one-day ultimatum to Germany demanding her withdrawal from Belgium.

Why?

Britain decided to uphold a treaty she had signed in 1839 respecting Belgium's neutrality. When no offer to withdraw was received from Germany by midnight, Britain entered war against her.

NO THOROUGHFARE

BRAVO, BELGIUM!

▲ A cartoon from *Punch* magazine, August 12, 1914

23

'Sacred love of the fatherland, Guide and support our vengeful arms.'	'Germany, Germany, over all, Over everything else in the world.'	'Land of hope and glory... God who made thee mighty, Make thee mightier yet!'
French national anthem	Unofficial German national anthem	British patriotic words to Elgar's music

Patriotism

Did the people of these countries accept the necessity of war?

There was an enormous amount of enthusiasm for this war. People instinctively wanted to preserve their homes and country from foreign invasions. They had a strong patriotic pride in their own country, whose virtues they felt were worth fighting for.

YOUR COUNTRY'S CALL

Isn't this worth fighting for?

ENLIST NOW

▲ Britain's green and pleasant land

Each country regarded itself as being superior to any other nation. Schoolchildren were taught to take pride in their historical tradition. Textbooks told of past national achievements and the glories of any colonial empire. In Germany, schoolboys – to prepare them for conscription – were encouraged to join a youth army, Jungdeutschlandbund. In this, physical fitness and patriotic values were fostered: 'War is beautiful... it will be more beautiful and more wonderful to live forever among the heroes of a war memorial in a church than to die an empty death in bed, nameless.'

The nearest organisation Britain had to a youth army was the Boy Scouts. Baden-Powell, its founder, saw the movement as a way of enabling the Empire to survive: 'We must stick shoulder to shoulder as Britons if we want to keep our present position among the nations. Play up! Play up! Each man in his place and play the game!'

For some in Britain, war was regarded as a glorious game. Youths and men from all classes of society were keen to volunteer for the British army. The popular press played on this patriotism. The *Daily Express* headline for August 5, 1914 was:

England Expects That Every Man Will Do His Duty.

ds, Sheffield, Birmingham, Hull, Barnsley (2), Liverpool (4), Salford, Accrington, Grimsby Chums,
ham Comrades, Stockbrokers', Glasgow Tramways, North Eastern Railway, 36th Ulster (division),
eside Irish (4), Tyneside Scottish (4)

ne Pals battalions

The British Expeditionary Force

What was the British army like in 1914?

Of its regular troops, about 120,000 soldiers were in the British Expeditionary Force (BEF) ready for action; the rest were overseas.

The BEF was an exceptionally well-trained army, particularly expert at rifle operations and recognised as being tactically outstanding.

Together with the reservists and Territorials, Britain could mobilise about 730,000 men, but, in comparison with other major powers, this was a modest contribution.

In August 1914 four of the six infantry divisions and the one cavalry division were sent to the Belgian border. These were joined in November by an Indian corps of two infantry and two cavalry divisions. The Secretary of State for War, Lord Kitchener, was one of the very few who predicted a war lasting for at least three years. He aimed to create an army of at least 60 infantry divisions by that third year. He appealed for volunteers for 'new armies'. By the end of 1914, 1,186,337 men had volunteered. After that, the number rarely dipped below 100,000 a month – about the size of the original BEF – and, by the end of 1915, 2,466,719 men had been accepted to fight for 'King and country'.

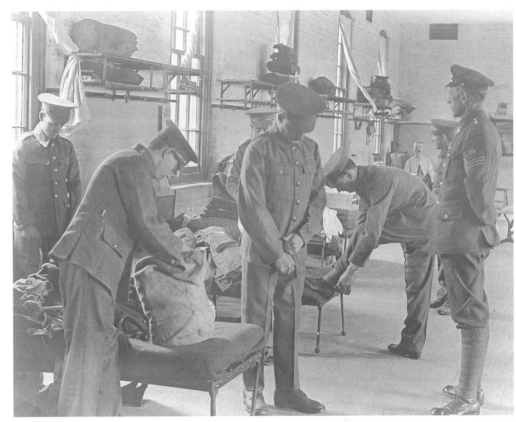

▲ The transformation from civilian to soldier

Volunteers were formed into battalions and absorbed into the existing army structure. Some battalions, known as Pals, consisted of men who worked and played together – in factories, as students, in football teams. This new mass army had to be equipped and trained as quickly as possible to take on the strongest military force in the world.

	Britain	France	Russia	Germany	Austria-Hungary	Italy
Infantry divisions	6	63	110	82	49	Declared itself neutral in 1914
Cavalry	1	10	36	11	11	
	Triple Entente (Allies)			Triple Alliance (Central Powers)		

The Imperial German Army

▲ The well-trained and well-equipped Germany infantry

What was the German army like in 1914?

Its regular troops numbered 700,000 men, and its land force was recognised as the most efficient in the world.

The German army was meticulously prepared for any tactical and supply eventuality. Its equipment was generally superior to that of its opponents. Germany, with the Kaiser as supreme war-lord, prided itself on its military culture. Within a week of mobilisation, 3.8 million men were under arms. The table below gives some idea of the strengths of the opposing Allies and Central Powers.

	1914 estimates	Population	Soldiers (regular and reserves)	Merchant ships	Warships (inc. under construction)	Submarines
ALLIES	Britain	46m	711,000	20.00m tonnes	122	64
	France	40m	1,250,000	2.00m tonnes	46	73
	Russia	167m	1,200,000	0.75m tonnes	26	29
CENTRAL POWERS	Germany	65m	2,200,000	5.00m tonnes	85	23
	Austria-Hungary	50m	810,000	3.00m tonnes	24	6

In addition, each country mobilised thousands of horses for cavalry and draught horses for artillery and transport waggons.

All nations had war plans in case of war. Germany was confident that hers, the Schlieffen Plan (named after its creator, a previous chief of general staff), would ensure that this war would be a short conflict. To avoid fighting on two fronts, the plan was to defeat France quickly in the west, then transport troops by rail to the east to defeat Russia. Speed was essential if France was to be defeated before Russia was fully mobilised. The Germans calculated that 40 days was all that was necessary to reach Paris and conquer the French. The Schlieffen Plan began well. Despite heroic resistance from the Belgians, by August 24 they had been crushed by the German advance.

many des ium	Germany advances through Belgium and northern France	German troops 40km from Paris	Battle of the Marne	Race to the sea	Trench warfare	First Battle of Ypres	Casualties: French 306,000 British 89,000 German 241,000 Belgian 30,000
4 August 3			September 5–10			October 15	By November

Schlieffen and stalemate

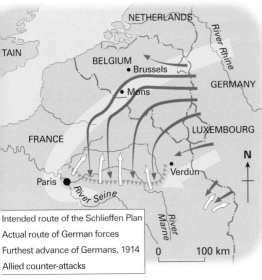

Intended route of the Schlieffen Plan
Actual route of German forces
Furthest advance of Germans, 1914
Allied counter-attacks

0   100 km

▲ The Schlieffen Plan and the actual route taken in 1914

What was the French war plan?

They used Plan 17 to launch a direct attack on Germany at the Alsace-Lorraine frontier on August 20.

In 12 days the French lost 200,000 men against artillery and machine-gun fire. Abandoning Plan 17, the French regrouped to defend Paris from the advancing Germans.

The BEF, after being shipped over to Boulogne, met the Germans at Mons on August 23. They achieved initial success, but, heavily outnumbered, had to organise an early retreat.

The Germans, however, began to face problems. Supplies could not keep up with their rapidly advancing men. They then had to pull out 100,000 troops to send to the east – Russia had mobilised more quickly than expected and had already invaded Germany. The Schlieffen Plan was then altered. German troops, instead of swinging around Paris, advanced straight towards it. The French transported soldiers by rail and even taxi to defend their capital. At the Battle of the Marne, combined French and British forces counter-attacked, pushing the Germans back to the River Aisne.

British forces
German forces
French forces
Fortress town
Front line in early 1915

▲ The 'race to the sea' and line of trenches

By September 8 both sides were digging trenches to protect themselves. The Germans tried to outflank enemy lines by charging west in a 'race to the sea' but were blocked at each attempt. At Ypres, Artois and Champagne neither side could break through gaps in the trenches. Stalemate set in. Millions of soldiers spent Christmas somewhere along a continuous line of trenches stretching from the North Sea to neutral Switzerland. This line became known as the Western Front.

The First World War

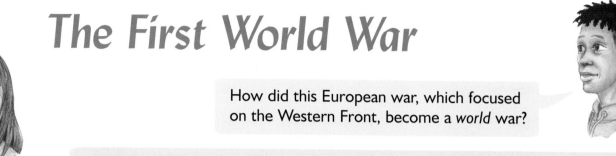

How did this European war, which focused on the Western Front, become a *world* war?

It was not just fought in Europe by Europeans. It involved all the Great Powers, and, as both the Allies and the Central Powers had overseas colonies in Africa, Asia and the Americas, fighting took place in some of these colonies.

It was also a world war where troops fought outside their own region for the first time. Americans and Canadians, for example, fought in France. Some of the main fronts are illustrated below.

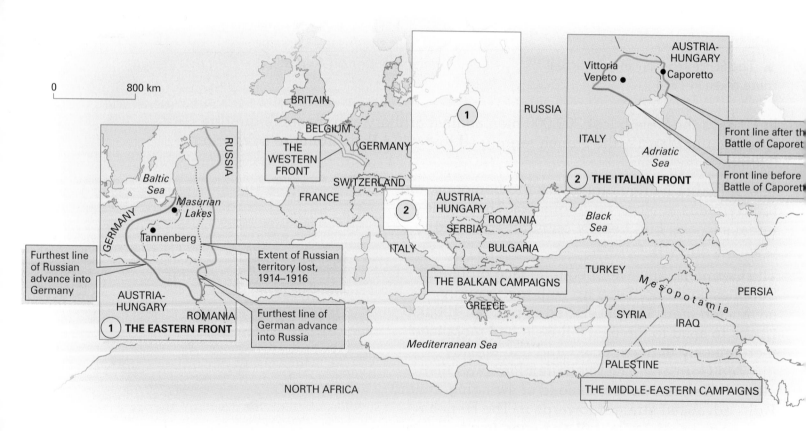

▲ ① The Eastern Front

In 1914 the Russians halted an Austrian advance and pushed the Austrians back into Germany. When the Germans transferred their troops, they crushed the Russians at Tannenburg and the Masurian Lakes. After some successes in 1916, by 1917 the Russians had lost 2 million men, and, at home, millions of people were dying of starvation.

▲ ② The Italian Front

Italy joined the Allies in 1915 and hoped to win territory from Austria-Hungary. It suffered a major defeat by the Germans at Caporetto in 1917, but in September 1918 it inflicted a crushing defeat on Austria-Hungary at Vittoria Veneto.

	New Zealand (including Maoris): 124,000 enlisted; 100,000 served overseas	Canada: 600,000 enlisted; 418,000 served overseas Newfoundland: 9,000	India: 1.3m served	Egypt: 120,000 volunteer labour corps	South Africa: 146,000 whites; 85,000 blacks in labour battalions	West Indies: 15,000 served overseas, of whom 2/3 Jamaican
...alia: ...,000 ...ed ...seas						

...port for Britain's army, navy and air force

Other campaigns

Britain came to rely increasingly on support from her colonies and dominions. Thousands of men from the British Empire volunteered and fought on the Western and other fronts worldwide.

Gallipoli

Here, the Australian and New Zealand Army Corps (Anzac) fought alongside Indian, British and French troops against the Turks (who had joined the Central Powers). The plan was to defeat Turkey so that the Allies could supply Russia through the Black Sea. Once Turkey was defeated, Allied troops could march through the Balkans and attack Austria-Hungary.

The first campaign, a naval one, was withdrawn after three Allied warships were sunk and others damaged in the Dardanelles.

The following land campaign on the Gallipoli peninsula, beginning in March 1915, was fought at Helles, Anzac (later named so) and Suvla. Commanders underestimated the defensive ability of the Turks. Severe casualties, intense summer heat that brought disease, and then bitter winter cold that led to frostbite, forced the withdrawal of over 100,000 troops by January 1916. This was generally recognised as a disastrous venture.

The Middle East

The Turks also threatened Britain's oil supplies in Persia (now Iran). Allied troops, chiefly Anglo-Indian, were sent to Mesopotamia and were joined by Australian and New Zealand troops in Palestine to push the Turks back.

Colonel T E Lawrence (Lawrence of Arabia) was also sent to Palestine to train Arab tribes in guerilla warfare. The Arabs sought independence from Turkey, so such a military alliance was useful to the Allies.

The Balkan Campaign

The Allies also fought in Salonika, Greece. In fact, the idea was to help Serbia defeat Austria and Bulgaria and create a new front against Germany. This, too, like the Middle Eastern campaign, was a long operation. The cost of maintaining armies worldwide was to prove crippling for all major powers involved.

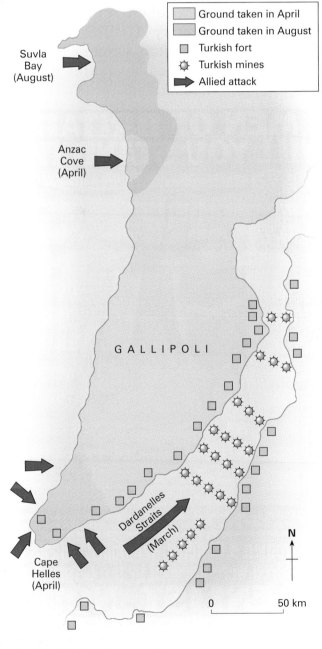

▲ The Gallipoli campaign

29

King George V changed name from Saxe-Coburg Gotha to Windsor	'God save our gracious King' played in theatres	Afternoon pub closing and beer watered down	Egg and chips popular – cheaper than meat	Paper banknotes replaced gold coins

Wartime innovations

7

The Home Front

Did civilians face attack in the First World War?

Yes, by sea and air.

The first civilian casualties occurred in Hartlepool, Scarborough and Whitby when German ships, lying offshore, shelled the north-east coast and more than 500 people were killed or injured. The first serious air raid using Zeppelin airships took place on January 20, 1915, when 20 bombs from 3 Zeppelins were dropped on Great Yarmouth, Cromer, Sheringham and inland at King's Lynn. These raids resulted in four deaths and the destruction of property. By 1917, after 57 raids, 564 people had been killed.

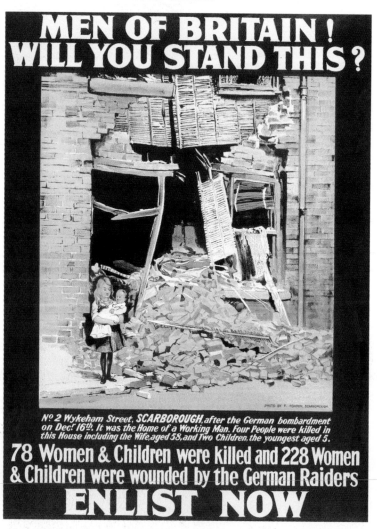

MEN OF BRITAIN! WILL YOU STAND THIS?

Nº 2 Wykeham Street, SCARBOROUGH, after the German bombardment on Decr 16th. It was the Home of a Working Man. Four People were killed in this House including the Wife, aged 58, and Two Children, the youngest aged 5.

78 Women & Children were killed and 228 Women & Children were wounded by the German Raiders

ENLIST NOW

▲ A propaganda poster in response to German sea attacks

German aircraft (Gotha IV and Gigants) made 27 attacks, dropping 14,000 bombs over London and towns on the south coast. These resulted in 835 deaths and 2,000 injuries.

For defence, Britain had the Fleet to guard the east coast, barrage balloons, intercepting fighter planes, searchlights and anti-aircraft guns. Zeppelins were easily spotted and, if hit, burst into flames, with little chance of survival for the crew.

Civilian lives were also affected by government powers under the Defence of the Realm Act (DORA). Factories and land were taken over for war production. Strikes were made illegal, and British Summer Time was introduced to allow more daylight for working. Travel was restricted, public holidays cancelled, and, in 1917, race meetings and Football League matches were suspended. Public parks were taken over for the growing of vegetables, as food supplies were threatened by a German blockade. Even feeding bread to pigeons was forbidden by law to prevent waste. In 1918 rationing was introduced. People were given a book of coupons allowing them to buy a certain amount of a product each week.

...ouraged morale further sacrifices	Inflamed feeling against the 'Hun'	Persuaded friends to join Allies	Used cinema to influence the masses

...poses of propaganda

The propaganda campaign

Food shortages led to a poster campaign to persuade people to grow their own vegetables and not waste food. This was one part of a propaganda campaign by the government.

Why did it need to conduct a propaganda campaign?

This was because, as war continued for so long, it was important to boost morale and encourage people to make sacrifices to help the war effort, especially after conscription was introduced in 1916.

Newspaper reports were censored. Air and sea raids were skilfully exploited to foster 'anti-Hun' (anti-German) attitudes. Aeroplanes dropped leaflets behind enemy lines to undermine German morale. Another way of spreading 'hate' propaganda was by word of mouth. Hostile and exaggerated rumours about the wickedness of the Hun were spread, and posters showing supposed acts of German brutality were printed. The government also spread friendly propaganda in the form of books and pamphlets, some in particular directed towards the USA. It was anxious to win over American public opinion for this war.

Was radio used?

This was not sufficiently developed yet, but cinema certainly was. By 1917 there were 4,500 cinemas in Britain.

People flocked to see cartoons poking fun at 'incompetent' Germans. They went to see films about a new weapon – the tank. Hundreds of thousands queued to see a film of one battle, the Somme. Made while the battle was in progress, it showed scenes of trench warfare and included dead and wounded soldiers. Though some scenes were posed, the audiences were impressed at the courage and cheerfulness of the British 'Tommy'.

▲ A propaganda appeal to civilians

31

Women at war

As men fought on the Western and other fronts, women worked at home and even behind the front lines to support the war effort. The campaign for the vote had been suspended. As Emmeline Pankhurst of the WSPU declared: 'What is the use of fighting for the vote, if we have not got a country to vote in?' It was Mrs Pankhurst who suggested that women should work in munitions factories, and she organised a procession to demand this right.

▲ 'Shells made by a wife may save her husband's life': an official war painting of a munitions factory

By 1918 over 750,000 women had been employed in munitions factories. With so many men absent at war, women began to enter the workforce in huge numbers, often taking over jobs which had previously been thought of as jobs only men could do. Women became road-sweepers, fire-fighters, chimney-sweeps, blacksmiths, bakers, grave-diggers and police-women. London County Council trained women to be plumbers and electricians, and, by 1916, all the Council's ambulances were staffed by women. Nearly 18,000 became 'Land Girls', part of the Land Army, working full-time on farms. With the help of 300,000 part-time workers, they ploughed, milked, weeded and carted grain. Many women joined the armed forces and worked as nurses, ambulance-drivers, telephonists, cooks and cleaners behind the lines.

Did men object?

Some male trade unionists were worried that men's wages would be lowered to match those of women (often paid less). Most men, however, were impressed by the contribution women made and became more aware that not allowing women the vote was an injustice.

British Grand Fleet:		BATTLE OF JUTLAND	German High Seas Fleet:	
Dreadnoughts	1 seaplane-carrier		16 Dreadnoughts	6 pre-Dreadnoughts
attlecruisers	1 minesweeper		5 battlecruisers	Submarine backup
rmoured cruisers	Submarine backup		11 light cruisers	2,551 sailors died
light cruisers	6,094 sailors died		61 destroyers	
destroyers				

1916 May 31

The war at sea

WAR AT SEA AND
8
IN THE AIR

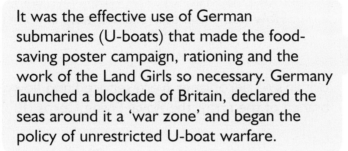

It was the effective use of German submarines (U-boats) that made the food-saving poster campaign, rationing and the work of the Land Girls so necessary. Germany launched a blockade of Britain, declared the seas around it a 'war zone' and began the policy of unrestricted U-boat warfare.

What was that?

The sinking of merchant ships without warning. Normally, the enemy allowed crew to take to boats, and provided them with food, water and a safe passage before sinking their vessel.

Now, U-boat captains used gunfire and torpedo at will. This led to a diplomatic crisis when, in May 1915, the U-20 fired on the British liner, *Lusitania*. A single torpedo sank the ship in 18 minutes, resulting in the loss of over 1,000 passengers, including 128 Americans. The resulting outcry, particularly from the USA, led to Germany imposing strict limitations on its submarine activity. Meanwhile Britain, using its Grand Fleet cruisers, destroyers and submarines, kept up its own blockade of Germany.

In 1916 the Germans decided to risk taking all its High Seas Fleet into the North Sea to engage the Grand Fleet in the one major naval battle of the war. In the resulting Battle of Jutland, Germany lost fewer ships, but many of those remaining suffered heavy damage. Forced to return to harbour, they did not dare venture outside coastal waters again. For the time being, Britain could sustain its blockade. This prevented German trade with the world outside Europe.

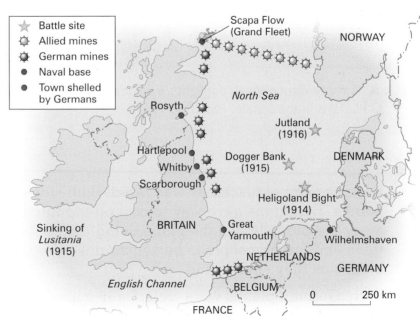

▲ War in the North Sea

Eddie Rickenbacker (American): 26 victories – survived	Major Edward 'Mick' Mannock (British): 73 victories – killed	Captain Albert Ball (British): 43 victories – killed	Baron Manfred von Richthofen (German): 80 victories – killed	Rene Fonck (French): 75 victories – surviv

Air aces

Aeroplane warfare

How many planes were available in 1914?

Britain's 63 aeroplanes were serviced and flown by men from a branch of the army, the Royal Flying Corps (RFC).

▲ A three-dimensional 'dogfight', a painting by G H Davis in the *Sphere*, March 1, 1919

The navy also had a flying branch, the Royal Navy Air Service (RNAS), which controlled all airships and maintained the defence of British airspace. One of the main tasks of RFC planes was reconnaissance. Pilots flew over enemy lines to take photographs that provided information about the movement of enemy troops, the position of heavy guns and trench defences. 'Dogfights' developed when German pilots tried to shoot down reconnaissance planes.

Early machines were crude and flimsy. Pilots sat in open cockpits with only goggles, leather helmets and thick coats for protection against cold and bullets. Bombs were dropped over the side by hand. With no parachute or radio, few navigational instruments and just a handgun for a weapon, the average fighting life of a pilot in 1917 was two weeks.

Development of machines was rapid. Both sides developed planes that could carry bombs. Handguns gave way to cockpit-mounted machine-guns. As these at first shot away the propellers of the plane doing the shooting, a new invention allowed the guns and the propellers to be synchronised so that bullets could be fired between the blades as they spun round.

Early German planes were technically superior. It was the arrival of planes such as the Bristol Fighter, SE-5A, Sopwith Camel and Triplane, and Handley Page 0/400 that established Britain's eventual technical superiority. When the Royal Air Force was formed by amalgamating the RFC and RNAS in 1918, it could soon boast over 22,000 aeroplanes.

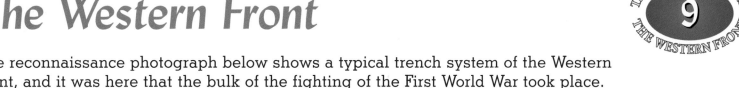

	Corps 3–4 divisions	Division 4 battalions	Battalion 4 companies	Company 4 platoons	Platoon 4 sections	Section 8–10 men	BEF had 5 armies. Precise numbers depended on army's role.
t 100,000 men. → rps.							

4 British Expeditionary Force   By 1918

The Western Front

The reconnaissance photograph below shows a typical trench system of the Western Front, and it was here that the bulk of the fighting of the First World War took place. This was where the British and French fought for total victory against Germany; and this is where thousands of men from both sides died in the struggle to achieve it.

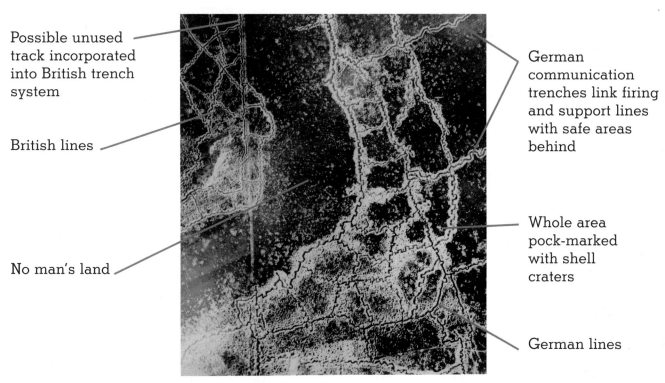

Possible unused track incorporated into British trench system

British lines

No man's land

German communication trenches link firing and support lines with safe areas behind

Whole area pock-marked with shell craters

German lines

▲ The German trench system between Loos and Halluch, as seen from the air. This British reconnaissance photograph was taken at 7.15pm on July 22, 1917.

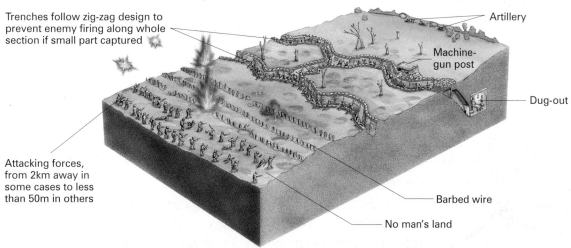

Trenches follow zig-zag design to prevent enemy firing along whole section if small part captured

Artillery

Machine-gun post

Dug-out

Attacking forces, from 2km away in some cases to less than 50m in others

Barbed wire

No man's land

▲ A cross-section of the trench system. A platoon of up to about 45 men would be stationed along a section of trench.

1914–1918

Trench life

What was the routine in the trenches?

Every month a front-line soldier might expect to spend eight days in the front trench, eight days in reserve in case of enemy attack, and the remaining time away from the front in a town or village.

When no battles were being fought, time was divided between sentry duty, trench maintenance, rifle cleaning and fetching supplies. Food was predictable – usually beef, biscuits and jam. Life at times could be tedious and dull. Washing facilities were scarce and sewerage systems crude. Conditions could be squalid.

The stench, particularly in summer when corpses were rotting, hung heavy in the air. In winter, after standing long hours in the cold and wet, the soldiers' feet swelled inside their boots. As circulation was cut off, the feet began to rot into a condition called 'trench foot' – often toes had to be amputated. All soldiers were infested with lice which incubated their eggs in body heat. The most detested of all vermin was the rat. Soldiers shot, bayoneted, clubbed and poisoned these loathsome creatures that thrived on dead human flesh. The corpses of comrades offered plenty.

All soldiers knew that at any time they could be required to go 'over the top' of the trench into no man's land. Some suffered terrible mental torture in this war. It took great mental and physical courage to face what all knew was a cruel lottery – that of life or death.

▲ *Over the Top*, a painting by John Nash

enades: one-shot bombs rown by hand or fired from e; had timed fuse for tonation or relied on impact	Rifles: accurate aim; 600-metre range; skilled riflemen could fire 15 rounds a minute	Shells: some smoke-filled to conceal troop movements	Mortars: high-trajectory artillery for close-range attack

No man's land

Why was no man's land called this?

It was the disputed territory between the front-line trenches of opposing armies. It belonged to no man until it was fought over and won.

In daytime it was often eerily silent, with little movement. At night there could be intense activity. Wiring parties would venture out to improve defences, patrols would crawl out to reconnoitre, and the occasional raiding party would swoop out of nowhere, killing as many of the enemy as possible and seizing prisoners for interrogation.

It was also the scene of major assaults. Attackers, using artillery, long-range heavy field-guns and howitzers, bombarded the enemy trenches. Shells included shrapnel that exploded into fragments

▲ A German G8 machine-gun, which could fire between 300 and 450 rounds a minute

and thousands of metal pellets which pierced the flesh. The most destructive were those filled with high explosive (HE). After such a 'barrage' by their own artillery behind them, the attackers scrambled up the sides of their trenches and 'over the top' to advance. It then became a race between them and the defenders, who had to emerge from their trenches and fire before the attackers got over the barbed wire and tackled them at close quarters. Defenders in this sort of situation usually had the advantage because each machine-gun had the estimated power of between 60 and 100 rifles, releasing eight or more bullets a second. Whole brigades could be, and were, wiped out in minutes. The aim was to send enough soldiers 'over' so that some would remain alive to secure enemy trenches. Over time, no man's land became a scrapyard of metal debris and a graveyard of human remains.

British weapon production

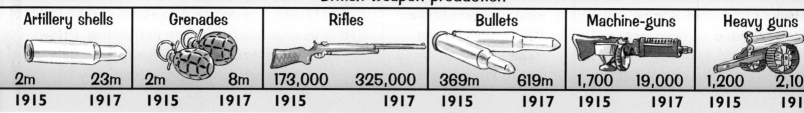

Artillery shells		Grenades		Rifles		Bullets		Machine-guns		Heavy guns	
2m	23m	2m	8m	173,000	325,000	369m	619m	1,700	19,000	1,200	2,10(
1915	1917	1915	1917	1915	1917	1915	1917	1915	1917	1915	1917

New weapons: gas and flame-throwers

As both sides sought to improve the killing potential of existing weapons, they also experimented with new attacking ideas to break the frustrating deadlock of trench warfare. The use of gas was generally dismissed as being uncivilised, but the Germans did release lethal chlorine gas from cylinders in the second Battle of Ypres in April 1915. Carried by the wind, it caused total panic and terrible deaths from respiratory failure in seconds. The German troops, however, shocked by the destruction caused, failed to exploit the sudden gap in Allied lines. Despite protests from countries such as the USA, which was then neutral, the Germans continued with the use of gas.

▲ A gas attack. Note the stick grenade shown at the top left.

What did the Allies do?

They retaliated. The British used gas from September 1915.

The drawback of gas was the need for ideal weather conditions. If the wind changed direction, so did the gas. Gas in shells was more effective, and a variety of gases were used in this form. From September 1917, the Germans introduced the use of odourless mustard gas. This was particularly insidious as it delayed and masked symptoms such as vomiting or internal and external blistering, often leading to death. Gas masks, at first primitive, soon became an effective deterrent.

There was no deterrent against another new weapon – the hand-held flame-thrower. The Germans used this as standard from July 1915. In this weapon, oil was forced through a nozzle and ignited by a spark to create a sheet of flame. One British eyewitness of an attack said that men caught in the direct blast of the fire 'were never seen again'.

tanks at ttle of Somme	8 crew, commander used megaphone, 4 gunners, 1 driver, 2 gearsmen, hand signals to change gear	Tank Corps: 136 tanks	378 tanks	Whippet tank: could travel at 12kph	534 tanks at Battle of Amiens
16 September 15		1917 July 27	November 20	1918 spring	August 8

New weapon: the tank

Because of its limited range, the flame-thrower became a defensive, not an offensive, weapon. The search was on for a mobile weapon to support infantry attacks. It would need to be armoured against machine-gun fire and able to move through mud, across shell holes and trenches and over barbed wire. Thus the tank was born.

When Kitchener saw an early tank he dismissed it as a 'pretty mechanical toy'. Others, including Churchill and Lloyd George, thought otherwise, and 49 Mark 1 tanks were launched amid great expectations on September 15, 1916, during the Battle of the Somme. They did inspire immediate terror amongst the Germans, but, at this stage, did little else. Seventeen tanks failed to reach German lines and, of the 32 that crossed, 14 were either ditched, broke down or shelled. Nevertheless, their potential was recognised and more were ordered.

Did the Germans retaliate by building their own?

Surprisingly, they concentrated on ways to deal with British ones, building only twenty of their own (AVT) design.

▲ A Mark 1 tank, complete with wire box to prevent grenades being thrown in. The rear wheels were the steering gear.

Tanks certainly had teething problems. Travelling at less than 8kph, they were useless in retreat. Poor visibility, unreliability, excessive heat and noxious fumes inside created difficulties. Noise made communications difficult. On only two days during the war could the British army field a significant number of tanks, and, of the 534 fielded at the Battle of Amiens in 1918, only six were available on the fourth day. Eventually, however, the tank was to prove a key weapon in 20th-century offensive warfare.

| Generals used telephones to control battle up to their own front lines | In battle, telephone cables were destroyed; communication difficult | It took 8–10 hours for message to reach front from divisional headquarters | Runners, carrier-pigeons, dogs, signal-lamps, spotter aircraft – all haphazard |

Communications

The Front Line, 1914–1917

The trench system was established by the end of 1914. The front-line soldier might be called on to defend a quiet section of trench or be involved in one of the major battles of 1914 to 1917.

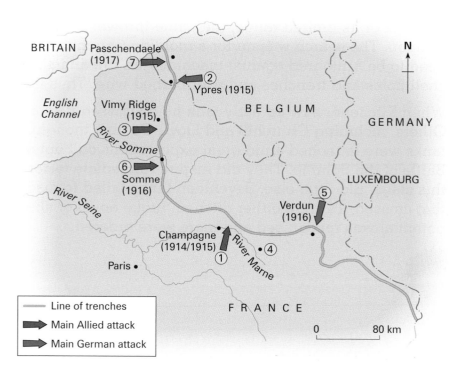

▲ The major battles on the Western Front, 1914–1917

Date	Battle	Main features	Casualties
December 1914 to March 1915	① Champagne	First, mainly French, offensive; territorial gain of 2km	90,000 French, incomplete German figures
April to May 1915	② Second Battle of Ypres	First use of gas by Germans; only major attack on Western Front by Germany this year	70,000 Allies, 35,000 Germans
May to November 1915	③ Vimy Ridge	Had been occupied by Germans from September 1914; tactically important ridge; repeated French attempts to take ridge failed	150,000 Allies, incomplete German figures
September 1915	④ Champagne	Second, mainly French, offensive; no strategic gains	145,000 French, 50,000 Germans
February to December 1916	⑤ Verdun	Longest battle in war; 1 million German troops versus about 200,000 French defenders; Germans gained a few kilometres; both sides suffered terrible losses	550,000 French, 434,000 Germans
July to November 1916	⑥ Somme	British diversionary attack from Verdun; first use of tank; British volunteer mass army shattered; Germany lost junior officers and experienced NCOs	420,000 British, 200,000 French, 500,000 Germans
July to November 1917	⑦ Third Battle of Ypres: Passchendaele	Ypres Salient widened a few kilometres by British; Canadians captured fortified Vimy Ridge; final offensive at Cambrai	310,000 British, 300,000 Germans

The Somme

Why is it that when the First World War is mentioned, it is the Battle of the Somme that most people seem to have heard of?

It was the first time tanks were used and the first time the large-scale use of the artillery tactic 'creeping barrage' was tried. In this, a carefully targeted artillery barrage enabled the infantry to inch forward in stages.

This battle is also remembered because of the conditions. Veterans thought that the mud, a glutinous quicksand in which men drowned in minutes, was the worst of the war.

However, the main reason people remember this battle is that between July and November 1916 it effectively destroyed the mass volunteer 'new armies' of 1914. On the first day, July 1, after a preliminary Allied bombardment of enemy positions over 7 days – and after being assured that there would not even be a rat alive in the enemy trenches – thousands of men were cut down over no man's land as they advanced.

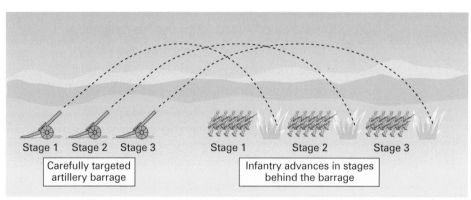

Stage 1   Stage 2   Stage 3   Stage 1   Stage 2   Stage 3

Carefully targeted artillery barrage

Infantry advances in stages behind the barrage

▲ Creeping barrage

The Pals Battalions – those which had been permitted to train and fight together – now died together, devastating local communities at home. The Tyneside Irish Brigade of four battalions, totalling nearly 3,000 men, lost 500 killed and wounded in one battalion and 600 in another. Of the 100,000 men who attacked that day, 20,000 never returned. The Somme campaign had the unhappy distinction of being recorded in the *Guinness Book of Records*:

> The battle with the greatest recorded number of military casualties [dead, wounded or missing] was the First Battle of the Somme, France from 1 July to 19 Nov. 1916, with 1,043,896 – Allied 623,907 (of whom 419,654 were British) and 419,989 German.

▲ Letters and personal belongings from the packs of the Somme dead and wounded being sent home (note the Model T Ford ambulances)

U-boats and the USA

The Germans, too, had suffered terribly and did not want their men to face 'Somme fighting' again. They decided, at the risk of causing another diplomatic crisis with the USA, to resume their policy of unrestricted submarine warfare from February 1, 1917.

Was it successful?

Yes, very. By this time, with over 100 U-boats, they were certain they could starve Britain into defeat. German naval staff estimated that if 600,000 tonnes of Allied shipping were sunk a month, Britain could be brought to starvation levels in five months. By April they had begun to exceed this target. Soon Britain had only enough food left for six weeks. The Admiralty were reluctantly persuaded to use the convoy system.

What was that?

A group of between 10 and 15 camouflaged merchant ships, often with a troop ship in its midst, was guarded at the front, rear and flanks by warships, chiefly destroyers.

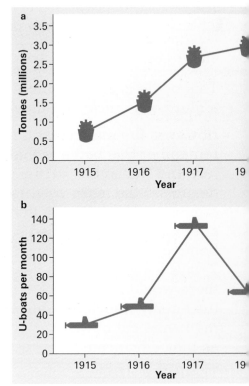

▲ **a** Tonnage of British shipping lost
b Average number of U-boats in action

▲ American convoy bringing troops to France, 1918

At the back of the convoy, torpedo boats had aerial balloons attached, which enabled observers to look down from baskets to detect underwater U-boats or passing torpedoes. Depth charges could then be dropped. This system transformed the war at sea. In July and August, out of 800 ships travelling in convoy, 15 were sunk. In all, out of 16,000 merchant ships using the convoy system, only 154 were sunk. Convoys also carried American troops because, after the sinking of three American merchant ships by the Germans in March, America decided to enter the war on April 6, 1917.

-day eliminary mbardment	Opening assault at Pickem Ridge. 3rd Battle of Ypres (Passchendaele)	Langemarck: tiny British gains, heavy casualties	Menin Road Bridge	Polygon Wood and Broodseinde established British position on ridge east of Ypres
17 July 16	July 31	August 16	September 20	September 26 to October 4

Passchendaele

Despite misgivings from Lloyd George, the then Prime Minister, Field Marshal Sir Douglas Haig, Commander in Chief of the BEF, persisted in another major offensive in July 1917, employing similar tactics to those used on the Somme. His meticulous preparations did not allow for relentless rain, or the fact that the drainage system of the low-lying fields of Flanders had been destroyed. Here again, the ground became a sludge of porridge-like mud. At times more men drowned in the mud than were shot.

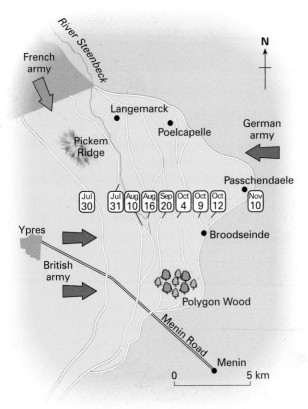

▲ *The Menin Road* by Paul Nash, a painting of the Passchendaele battlefield

The horrors of this battle, like others, were recorded not just by statistics, reports and photographs. Men who fought also painted and composed poetry. They wanted to capture the reality of war. Paul Nash, after being wounded in 1917, returned as an official war artist. His work, he said, 'will have a bitter truth'.

The writer Siegfried Sassoon composed this poem:

I died in hell –
(They called it Passchendaele): my wound was slight,
And I was hobbling back, and then a shell
Burst slick upon the duckboards, so I fell
Into the bottomless mud, and lost the light.

Between July 27 and November 20 those who 'lost the light' in this battle were estimated at 265,423 British and 206,000 Germans.

For Lloyd George, Passchendaele was the battle 'which, with the Somme and Verdun, will always rank as the most gigantic, tenacious, grim, futile and bloody fight ever waged in the history of the war'.

The British gained 11km of mud, but by this point in the war, though determined to fight to the bitter end, many soldiers had lost their optimism and hope, and despaired for the future.

▲ A map marking the change in the front line after Passchendaele

One letter, Passchendaele

▲ Private Jack Mudd

John William (Jack) Mudd was a Cockney from Bow in the East End of London. In 1917 he was 31 years old and married with a family. His wife, Elizabeth, was generally known as Lizzie.

On October 26 that year, as a Private in the 2nd/4th Battalion, London Regiment, Royal Fusiliers, Jack Mudd took part in a dawn attack in the Ypres Salient as part of the Battle of Passchendaele. Four days before the assault he wrote this letter to his wife:

My darling Lizzie

At last I have the opportunity of writing to you a real letter. In the first place dearest I trust you and the children are quite well. I guess you have been worried with the air raids. You know dear it's hard to be out here fighting and yet your wife and children can't be safe. Still dearest don't worry, you have a 20,000 to 1 chance and God will watch over you as he has been with me ever since I have been out here. I have tried dearest to be as good as I can since I have been in France. I never close my eyes without praying for myself, you and the children. He has answered them up till now and I hope and trust it will please Him to look after us until the end.

We are expecting to go up again in 2 or 3 days, so dearest pray hard for me and ask Marie for God will not refuse her prayers, she doesn't know the wickedness of this world.

is my painful duty to inform you that no further news having been received relative to Private John
...lliam Mudd, the Army council have been regretfully constrained to conclude that he is dead.'

...my Form B. 104-82A, sent to Lizzie Mudd

One death, Passchendaele

Dear Lizzie it's nearly six months now since I saw you, how I long for you and the children, God bless you all. I love you more than ever. I long to take you in my arms again, what a lot of love we have missed but please God it will make it all the sweeter when I see you. I often take your Photo out of my pocket and look at your dear face and think of the times we have had together, some lovely days eh love, and when I think again of some of the worry I have caused you it makes me only the more eager to get home to you to atone for all the worry and anxious moments you have had to put up with. You always stuck by me in all things dear God bless you for it. And my dear little children, I think of them, God bless them also. I hope dear you will always trust in me for I am always faithful your face is always before me and I couldn't deny you and as for you dearest I know you are faithful and no matter what happened you would always be true and keep your word.

Out here dear we're all pals, what one hasn't got the other has, we try to share each others troubles, get each other out of danger. You wouldn't believe the Humanity between men out here. Poor little Shorty, one of the fellows that came out with me, he used to tell me all about his young lady, his Hilda, that was his young lady's name, about his home he had already bought and when he got home he would get married and come over to see me and introduce her to you. He used to make me laugh with his talk, how he loved his Hilda but unfortunately he will never see her again poor fellow, he would give me half of everything he had. I often think of him yet poor fellow I don't think he even has a grave but lies somewhere in the open. Still dear I don't want to make you sad but it just shows you how we seem to stick together in trouble. It's a lovely thing is friendship out here.

Please God it won't be long before this war is over, we are pushing old Fritz back, I don't think he will stand the British boys much longer and then we will try and keep a nice home. I will know the value of one now. Goodnight love God bless you and my children and may He soon send me back to those I love is the wish of Your Faithful Husband

xxxxxxxx Jack

▲ Lizzie Mudd

On October 26, after the raid, when the roll call was taken, Private Mudd was not among the survivors. His body, like that of nearly 35,000 others in this battle, was never found.

Tsar Nicholas II of Russia abdicates	USA declares war on Germany	Suspension of hostilities between Russia and Germany	Treaty of Brest-Litovsk between Central Powers and Russia	German offensive in Picardy begins	'Backs to the wall' order of the day by Haig
1917 March 15	April 6	December 2	**1918** March 3	March 21	April 12

THE END OF THE FIRST WORLD WAR **10**

The 1918 German offensive

If the USA entered the war in April 1917, why didn't she send men to fight at Passchendaele?

America's fleet was the second largest after Britain's, but her army of 108,000 men was ranked 17th in the world. Her best force, the Marines, numbered only 15,500.

▲ A propaganda postcard encouraging Americans to enlist

FOR FREEDOM!

Once she decided to enter the war, however, the USA moved quickly to organise troops. To raise numbers, conscription was introduced, and troops were already arriving in France by June 1917. By March 1918, 318,000 troops – protected by the convoy system – had reached there.

Germany, too, had extra men. She had been able to transport 50 infantry divisions from the east after the political collapse of Russia and her withdrawal from the war. With this unexpected resource and no further threat from Russia, the Germans planned a final offensive westwards before the bulk of Americans arrived.

With the emphasis on speed, Operation Michael was launched on March 21, 1918. Using chlorine and phosgene gas, and a barrage mixed with mustard gas, almost all British positions were overrun. Special German 'storm troop' units broke through defences. As the Germans pushed towards Amiens, they re-entered the area where the Battle of the Somme had taken place in 1916. German divisions, many of whose men were ill-fed, came across abandoned supplies of food. Hunger tempted them to loot and stop to eat and drink rather than press forward to fight. Delays were costly. When the Allies launched a counter-attack, the Germans lost about 250,000 men. The British and French could replace their lost men with fresh and enthusiastic Americans. German soldiers lost, however, were irreplaceable.

tle of Amiens: endorff, a German nmander, calls this black day for the man army'	Bulgaria signs armistice	Turkey signs armistice	Austria-Hungary signs armistice	Kaiser Wilhelm II abdicates	Armistice between Allies and Germany end hostilities
8 August 8	September 30	October 30	November 3	November 9	November 11

'Backs to the wall'

What did the Germans do?

They switched to a second offensive, Operation George, to reach the Channel ports behind Ypres. Again, the attack began well.

Haig issued a message to his second and first armies: 'With our backs to the wall... there will be no retirement.' With the help of tanks, the Germans were held. German troops then began to refuse to attack, despite orders. A third German offensive threatened Paris but French, British and American troops held firm. The German replacements were now 18-year-old conscripts and convalescents from hospital.

On August 8 the British and French, with 580 tanks and support from Canadians and Australians, launched a counter-attack. Then, on September 12, the first all-American offensive was launched. On September 26, after facing British, French, Belgian and American troops, the Germans began to seek an armistice (ceasefire). As fighting continued along the Western Front, Germany's allies signed their own respective armistices. Germany now stood alone. Her army had, by now, reached the limits of its endurance; furthermore her fleet had mutinied. On November 9, 1918 the Kaiser was forced to abdicate and the Germans agreed to sign an armistice. This took place in a railway carriage at Compiègne, near Paris, at the 11th hour of the 11th day of the 11th month – November 11, 1918. Lloyd George on that day spoke in the House of Commons: 'Thus, at eleven o'clock this morning came to an end the cruellest and most terrible war that has ever scourged mankind. I hope we may say that thus, this fateful morning came to end all wars.'

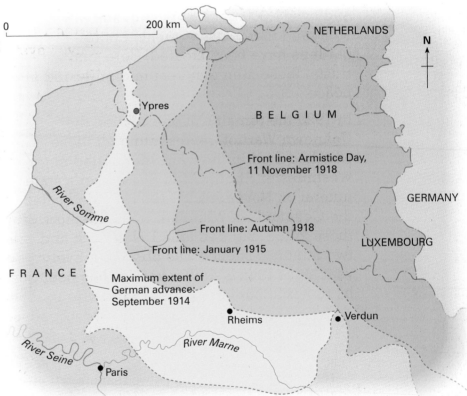

▲ The Western Front, 1914–1918

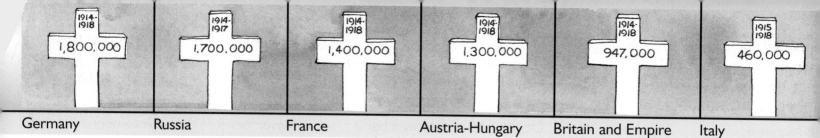

Germany	Russia	France	Austria-Hungary	Britain and Empire	Italy
1914-1918 1,800,000	1914-1917 1,700,000	1914-1918 1,400,000	1914-1918 1,300,000	1914-1918 947,000	1915-1918 460,000

Dignity in death

At the close of the war, the British chose to honour their dead in a unique way. In specially created cemeteries, each body was given its own grave. Headstones record the name, age, rank, regiment, and date and place of death if known. Space was left for relatives to add an epitaph. If the body was unidentifiable, the headstone was engraved with the words, 'A soldier of the Great War known unto God'. The names of those whose bodies were never found – over half of those killed – are recorded on monuments in these cemeteries.

More than 600 cemeteries were constructed and over 1,000 gardeners still, and always will, tend them. Over time, beautiful gardens have been created. Here, one trusts, these men may rest in dignity and at peace.

In 1920 the remains of one soldier, the Unknown Warrior, representing all those who had died in the war, were buried in Westminster Abbey. After the soldier's state funeral on November 11, the King dedicated the Cenotaph in Whitehall to the memory of those killed. Big Ben tolled 11 o'clock and two minutes' silence was observed. Every year since then a similar service has been held, accompanied by these words:

▲ Some of the 11,500 headstones at Tyne Cot British Military Cemetery and Memorial to the Missing in Belgium. Private Mudd's name can be found on the memorial here, together with the names of 34,887 others.

They shall grow not old, as we that are left grow old:
Age shall not weary them, nor the years condemn.
At the going down of the sun and in the morning
We will remember them.

▲ From *For the Fallen*, a poem by Laurence Binyon

epresentation of the People Act: tes for all men over 21 and omen over 30 if a householder married to one	No vote for prisoners, royalty or insane	Eligibility of Women Act: right to stand to become MPs	Equal Franchise Act: vote given to all women over 21

18 February

1928

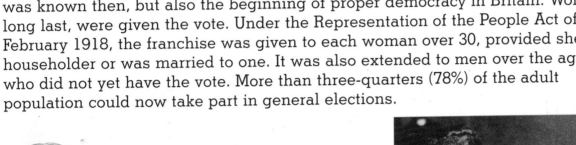

Democracy in Britain

11 PEACE-MAKING AND PEACE-KEEPING

The year 1918 marked not only the end of the First World War, or the Great War as it was known then, but also the beginning of proper democracy in Britain. Women, at long last, were given the vote. Under the Representation of the People Act of February 1918, the franchise was given to each woman over 30, provided she was a householder or was married to one. It was also extended to men over the age of 21 who did not yet have the vote. More than three-quarters (78%) of the adult population could now take part in general elections.

Is 'votes for all' an important part of democracy?

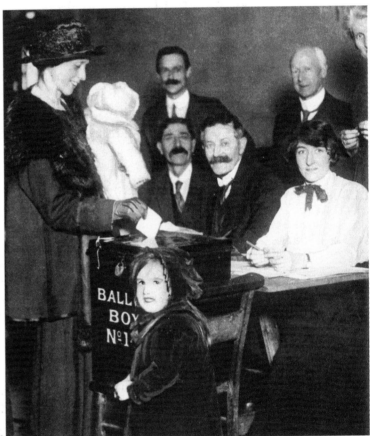

Yes, it is an *essential* feature in a democracy, as are the following:

• Every adult should be able to vote and help choose a government.

• Voters have the choice between several political parties.

• Governments stay in power for a limited time. After that, there must be another election.

▲ A woman voting during the general election, Saturday, December 14, 1918

• Everybody, including members of the government, must obey the laws of the land.

• Everybody has rights, such as the freedom to follow any religion, freedom to belong to a trade union, freedom of speech, freedom of opinion, and freedom of assembly. These freedoms are highly valued and are sometimes protected by law.

At the end of the Great War, President Wilson of the USA wanted to create a world safe for democracy. In January 1918 he proposed a programme of Fourteen Points, which he hoped would form the basis for discussions on the various armistices and peace treaties with Germany and the other defeated nations of Austria-Hungary, Turkey and Bulgaria. Wilson's ideal was to transform a world of war to one of peace and prosperity.

Wilson's Fourteen Points	No secret treaties	Free access to seas	Free trade between countries	Disarmament	Colonies to have say in own future	German troops to leave Russia	Independence for Belgium
	1	2	3	4	5	6	7

The 'Big Three'

Europe was in turmoil after the Great War. Land had been devastated, cultivation interrupted, railways destroyed and mines flooded. Populations, starved and weakened, were hit by an epidemic of influenza which killed thousands. Countries faced economic ruin and political chaos. The Russian, Hapsburg and Ottoman Empires had collapsed. The monarchs of the defeated powers had lost their thrones. Revolutions in Russia had resulted in the abdication of the Tsar and a new government hostile to the Allies.

Against this background of instability, the 'Big Three' – Wilson, Lloyd George and Clemenceau – met at Versailles in January 1919 for peace talks. Although they were united by the ideals of democracy, negotiations were not always cordial.

▲ Woodrow Wilson, President of the USA

Why was this?

▲ David Lloyd George, Prime Minister of Britain

Clemenceau, because France had suffered enormous damage during the war, was under tremendous pressure to deal harshly with Germany and thought Wilson and Lloyd George were too willing to appease her. He told Lloyd George that if Britain was so anxious to appease, they should offer Germany colonial, naval and commercial concessions. Lloyd George, not wanting Germany to keep her colonies and navy, as they remained a threat to Britain's Empire, resisted. Furthermore, both he and Wilson feared that if the terms of the Treaty were too harsh, Germany might one day recover and seek revenge by starting another war. There were other clashes. Clemenceau and Lloyd George, for example, thought that some of Wilson's Fourteen Points were unrealistic. Friction continued until June, when the Treaty was completed.

▲ Georges Clemenceau, Prime Minister of France

...rance ...o regain ...Isace-...orraine	Frontier between Austria and Italy adjusted	Self-determination for peoples of Eastern Europe	Turkey to have access to sea	Self-determination for peoples of Turkish Empire	Poland to be independent and have access to sea	League of Nations to be set up
8	9	10	11	12	13	14

The Treaty of Versailles

None of the 'Big Three' was satisfied with the finished Treaty. As a result, the map of Europe had to be redrawn.

a Land of North Schleswig given to Denmark after a vote.

b Land of Eupen and Malmédy given to Belgium.

c Germany not allowed to keep troops in the Rhineland, a border area between Germany and France.

d Saar controlled by League of Nations. Plebiscite (vote) after 15 years; coal to France for 5 years.

Legend:
- Newly independent states
- Land taken away from Germany
- Demilitarised zone
- Union forbidden

j Lithuania, Estonia and Latvia became independent states. Germany had taken these from Russia during the war.

i The port of Danzig became a 'free city'. It gave Poland a sea port.

h Poland given a 'Polish Corridor' to the Baltic Sea. This cut off East Prussia from Germany, splitting Germany in two.

g Part of Upper Silesia, an industrial area, given to Poland.

e Industrial area of Alsace-Lorraine, taken by the Germans in the 1870 Franco–Prussian War, to be given back to France.

f Germany forbidden to unite with Austria.

Did Germany agree to these changes to her frontier?

Germany was not consulted. Land terms, plus military and economic ones, were dictated terms she *had* to agree to.

Land terms

As well as loss of land in Europe, Germany lost all her colonies and all land gained from Russia.

Military terms

Army limited to 100,000 soldiers. Navy limited to six battleships. No submarines or armoured vehicles allowed. Air force disbanded. Rhineland demilitarised.

Economic terms

Under a 'war guilt' clause, Germany had to accept full responsibility for causing the war. She had to pay £6,600m in cash and materials (reparations) for damage done during the war.

1919 Effects of the Treaty of Versailles

German reaction to the Treaty

Did the Germans regard the Treaty as fair?

The people were shocked and outraged at the terms, which they saw as both severe and unfair.

PEACE AND FUTURE CANNON FODDER

The Tiger: "Curious! I seem to hear a child weeping!"

▲ A British cartoon of 1920. Clemenceau ('the Tiger') turns to see a child weeping. The child represents those who, by 1940, would be old enough to fight a war.

The 'war guilt' clause was particularly resented, as the Germans felt that they had not started the war and so should not take the blame for it. Many people, unaware of the military situation, felt that because they had not been defeated in their homeland, they had not lost the war. A ceasefire, they thought, meant that their government should have been included in the negotiations.

The people felt that it was not possible to pay the reparations demanded. The German economy was in ruins and people – faced with a continuing Allied blockade – were now dying of starvation.

Their economy would be weakened further by the loss of valuable industrial land and prestigious colonial territory. Another huge blow to the prestige of Germany was the forced reduction of her army to a mere 100,000 men. Germany had always prided herself on her military prowess. Her navy scuttled its ships in protest. Ebert, the new leader of the social democratic government, at first refused to sign the Treaty but, realising that Germany would lose if she chose to fight again, reluctantly did so. Many of his countrymen, particularly ex-soldiers, never forgave Ebert for what they thought was a betrayal of the Kaiser's Germany.

st 5 treaties med after jal chateaux d parks in ris area	Treaty of Versailles: Germany	Treaty of St Germain: Austria	Treaty of Neuilly: Bulgaria	Treaty of Trianon: Hungary	Treaty of Sèvres: Turkey	Treaty of Lausanne: Turkey – terms improved
	1919 June 28	September 10	November 27	**1920** June 4	August 10	**1923** July 2

Other peace treaties

Germany's resentment grew when she realised that, under the terms of the Treaty of Versailles and the other peace treaties that followed, German-speaking people were, without consultation, being placed in newly created countries. Whilst these countries were given self-determination (self-rule) as proposed in Wilson's Fourteen Points, millions of Germans were now to be governed by non-Germans.

Treaty of St Germain
Austria and Hungary separate countries. Parts of the old Hapsburg Empire given to Italy, Poland and Romania. Austria forbidden to unite with Germany. Army limited to 30,000 men and reparations to be paid.

Treaty of Sèvres
Not recognised by Turkish nationalists. After their military successes, this Treaty was replaced by Treaty of Lausanne. This returned most of European lands given away in earlier Treaty. No reparations paid.

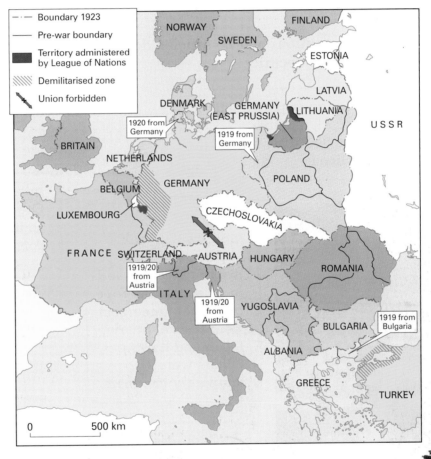

Treaty of Trianon
Hungary lost 2/3 of inhabitants and almost 3/4 of territory to Romania, Czechoslovakia and Yugoslavia. Army limited to 35,000 men and reparations to be paid.

Treaty of Neuilly
Bulgaria lost land to Greece and Yugoslavia. Army limited to 20,000 men and reparations to be paid.

Which were the new countries?

The countries created or recreated were Yugoslavia, Poland and Czechoslovakia.

As well as Czechs and Slovaks, Czechoslovakia contained Germans, Poles and Hungarians. Hungarians found themselves in Romania and Yugoslavia as well as Czechoslovakia. About 30 per cent of Poland's population were now not Polish. It included Russians, Jews, Germans and many others. President Woodrow Wilson's hope that ethnic-linguistic groups should rule themselves proved, in practice, to be impossible. Germany was also insulted by not being invited to join the League of Nations proposed by Wilson in the last of his Fourteen Points.

The League of Nations

Why was the League of Nations set up?

It was to be a permanent and international peace-keeping organisation. Its aim was to settle disputes between countries through discussion and negotiation.

Its covenant (constitution) had 26 articles designed to foster international co-operation, peace and security.

Assemby The League's parliament met once a year. All member nations voted on decisions, which had to be unanimous.

Secretariat The League's civil service

International Labour Organisation (ILO) To improve working conditions

Council A smaller group which took key decisions. Met five times a year and in emergencies. Four permanent members were France, Britain, Japan and Italy. Others were temporary members.

Court of International Justice Dealt with legal disputes between countries

▲ The Assembly Room of the League's headquarters at Geneva, Switzerland, a neutral country

Commissions and committees, e.g. the Mandates Commission. Many of the former colonies of Germany and her Allies were ruled by Britain and France on behalf of the League and were now called mandates. The Commission made sure this was done fairly.

The League had 45 founder members but the US Congress (parliament) tired of the friction during the peace process, and, despite the fact that the League was President Wilson's idea, voted against joining. This was a major blow to the League, as it could not really claim to speak for the world as a whole. Nevertheless, during the 1920s the League's commissions and committees had some notable successes in their aim to fight poverty, disease and injustice throughout the world. The Health Committee, for example, worked to defeat leprosy, malaria, cholera, dysentery and smallpox. The first Commissioner for Refugees, Nansen, organised the Nansen passport, which gave refugees a legal identity and a right to travel to look for work. The ILO's initiatives included limiting working hours for children.

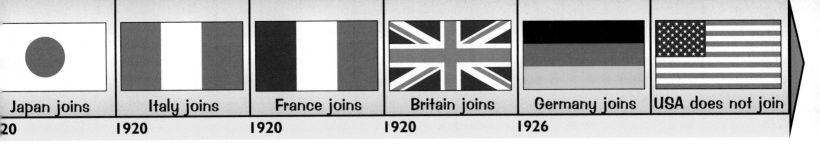

The League in the 1920s

In political matters progress was much slower, but many people saw grounds for optimism in the various agreements.

Some successes

Aaland Islands Both Sweden and Finland were threatening to fight over control of these islands midway between their two countries. They appealed to the League, which decided in favour of Finland. Sweden accepted the decision.

Upper Silesia Both Germany and Poland wanted control of this region on the border between them. A plebiscite (vote) was held: the industrial areas voted mainly for Germany; the rural areas mainly for Poland. The League divided the region along these lines and built in safeguards such as rail links to prevent further disputes. The decision was accepted by both countries.

Greece and Bulgaria A Greek army invaded Bulgaria after a border incident. The League ordered the Greeks to withdraw. Faced with disapproval from the major powers, Greece obeyed.

Mosal Both Iraq and Turkey claimed this region with its rich oilfield, formerly part of the Ottoman Empire. The League decided this frontier dispute in favour of Iraq, a British mandate.

1920
1921
1922
1923
1924
1925
1926
1927
1928
1929

Some failures

Vilna Poland captured Vilna, the capital of Lithuania. The League demanded Poland should hand Vilna back. Poland did not withdraw. The League failed to act and Poland kept Vilna.

Corfu incident Three Italian army officers were shot while working on a boundary dispute between Greece and Albania (Albania was under Greek protection). Italy, under Mussolini, blamed the Greeks and demanded compensation. When the Greeks refused to pay, the Italians occupied Corfu. Greece appealed to the League but the Italian government ignored its Council's ruling in Greece's favour. The Italians left Corfu only when the Greeks had paid compensation.

The USA

THE USA,
12
1918-1939

If the USA had joined the League of Nations, wouldn't it have become more involved in world affairs?

That is what, before his retirement through ill-health in 1919, President Wilson of the Democratic Party had hoped for, but what the other main political party, the Republicans, did not want.

▲ The United States of America

The 13 British colonies up to 1774

In the Presidential election campaign of 1920, Warren Harding, the successful Republican candidate, promised a return to 'normalcy' after Wilson's 'experiment' in Europe. By 'normalcy' Harding meant a return to the policy of isolation that America had followed before the First World War.

As a rich country, America could afford to be isolated. It had vast reserves of raw materials such as coal and oil so did not need to import many. It had a growing population which provided a strong home market, so did not need to export all its manufactured goods.

The industrial revolution in the USA of the late 19th century, which was based on coal, had brought steam engines, railways and mechanisation and had rapidly helped to make the USA the world's leading industrial power in most fields.

The First World War had sparked off another industrial revolution, this time based on electricity and oil. The USA was able to profit from sales of munitions, arms and foodstuffs to the Allies, and, while the warring nations were occupied, was able to take over their world trade. Wartime demands led to the development of new materials such as bakelite, rayon and cellophane, and had brought innovations such as automatic switchboards, power-shovels and dumper-trucks.

Post-war America benefited from these 'new' industries, the modernised older ones and a mass market.

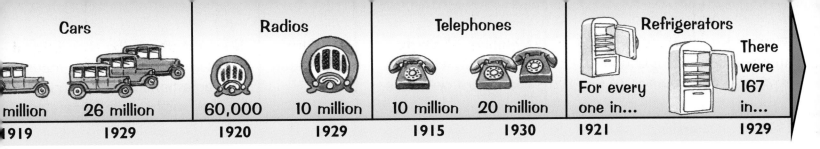

Cars		Radios		Telephones		Refrigerators	
						For every one in...	There were 167 in...
million	26 million	60,000	10 million	10 million	20 million		
1919	1929	1920	1929	1915	1930	1921	1929

Economic boom

To boost the economy, the Republicans – unlike the Democrats – favoured a policy of non-intervention (laissez-faire) in the everyday lives of American people. They felt that prosperity was arrived at by giving Americans the freedom to create wealth.

To protect businessmen from foreign competition, Harding introduced import tariffs which made foreign goods expensive. At the same time taxes were kept low to encourage people to buy home-produced goods and invest in companies.

Jobs were protected by the introduction of an immigrant quota in 1921, which restricted the number of people entering the country.

Did these policies work?

For many Americans, though by no means all, the 1920s did bring increased prosperity.

At the centre of this economic boom was the motor car industry. The 'great multitude' loved their Tin Lizzies. By 1927, one Model T Ford was rolling off the assembly lines every ten seconds. The industry directly and indirectly boosted employment in others such as paint, rubber and leather. Cars needed roads and roads led to new suburbs, creating more work for the construction industry, which in turn brought more businesses and more homes. Mass production techniques were used to make consumer goods to fill these buildings – furniture, vacuum cleaners, washing machines and so on. People were encouraged to buy these through mass nationwide advertising campaigns on radio, billboards, in the cinema and press and through travelling salesmen. Mail order increased markets and hire-purchase schemes were readily available. People even took out bank loans to buy shares in companies, confident of selling them at a profit. Americans, indeed, began to feel that prosperity was theirs by right.

▲ The cycle of prosperity

| Film censor appointed | No kiss to last longer than 2.13 metres of film | Members of clergy not to be used as comic characters or villains | Nudity forbidden | No sympathy to be shown to murder, safe cracking or arson, and acts not to be shown in detai as they might tempt amateurs |

1922 Film censorship

The Roaring Twenties

▲ Flappers dancing the Charleston in New York, 1926

The car helped to open up a suburb outside Los Angeles which enjoyed year-round sunshine – Hollywood. The film industry that developed there now led the world, gave employment to thousands and entertainment to millions who flocked to cinemas to see adventure stories, comedy films, cartoons and, most popular of all, romances. Stars, many presented as sex symbols, were swooned over. People copied their lifestyles – the cigarette-smoking, how to mix cocktails, the correct cutlery to use, the moustache, the glamorous clothes.

In 1930, 100 million Americans went 'to the movies' each week. Whilst films were 'silent' until 1927, radio was enthralling listeners with the sound of 'new' music, the blues and jazz. Dance bands were popular, too, accompanying energetic new dances such as the Black Bottom and the Charleston, and joining in the fun were the 'flappers'. With bobbed hair dyed black, tight felt hats, dresses that edged immodestly above the knee, silk stockings, bangles and beads, these fashionable young women became symbolic of the 'Jazz Age'. Defying convention, they wore make-up and smoked in public, rode motorbikes and went, without chaperones, for all-night drives in motor cars.

The car ferried young people to nightclubs, dance halls, sporting events and picnic spots away from the moral supervision of parents. Many of the older generation and those in the more conservative rural states thus came to deplore what they saw as the evils of modern city life. They felt that family life, religion and traditional American values were threatened by these new freedoms. One evil they had already campaigned to stamp out was the sale of alcohol.

ti-Saloon ague	Women's Christian Temperance Movement	18th Amendment to Constitution	Volstead Act: Prohibition	'Bootleggers': 17th-century word for smuggling bottles inside long leather boots	'Speakeasies' ('speak quietly'): illegal bars	'Moonshine': illegally brewed alcohol
60s		1918	1920 January			

Prohibition and crime

It was mainly religious groups which, sincerely believing that alcohol (liquor) would lead to a breakdown of society, led the Prohibition campaign. By 1917, 18 of the 48 states had banned alcohol and the First World War triggered further support.

Industrialists, preferring sober employees, backed the campaign. Politicians, needing the Prohibitionists' vote, supported them. Because the main brewers were German immigrants, people were persuaded that drinking beer was treasonable!

As a result, in 1918 the 18th Amendment to the Constitution stated that 'the manufacture, sale or transportation of intoxicating liquors... is hereby prohibited'. This became law in 1920, but only about 3,500 Prohibition Agents were appointed to enforce it.

Was the law broken?

In a country of about 100 million people, the law was easily ignored.

▲ Emptying beer kegs

Secret drinking dens (speakeasies) replaced saloon bars. Alcohol was illegally manufactured (moonshine). Smuggling (bootlegging) by sea and across the Mexican and Canadian borders was rife. It was the gangsters who, in addition to other rackets they ran such as gambling and vice, profited the most from Prohibition.

They bought up breweries, distilleries and speakeasies, and smuggled in alcohol in bulk. Hand- and machine-guns helped to guard consignments and were used in shoot-outs against rival gangs.

The most notorious Prohibition incident was the St Valentine's Day Massacre of 1929, when seven members of one Chicago bootleg gang were murdered by four from another. The main suspect for this and other murders was Al Capone, a well-known gang leader, but – as a friend of local police chiefs and politicians – he escaped prosecution, though he was eventually jailed for tax evasion. Prohibition mainly succeeded in bringing the law into disrepute.

The 'melting pot'

▲ Immigrants entering the USA in about 1900

Alfonso Capone was the son of Italian immigrants and Henry Ford the son of an Irish immigrant and his Dutch wife. These American citizens were part of the vast 'melting pot' of different races, cultures and religions that made up the vibrant society that was the USA.

The established immigrants, mostly White, Anglo-Saxon Protestants (WASPs), tended to look down upon the 13 million 'new' immigrants, many from Eastern Europe, who entered the country between 1900 and 1914.

The First World War led to immigrants from the Central Powers being regarded with suspicion and the Russian Revolution of 1917 brought fears of a communist take-over. The quota system of 1921, which protected jobs, restricted entry by allowing people into the USA only in proportion to the number of their nationality already in the country.

Didn't this mean that more Western Europeans than those of other nations could enter?

Yes, as they already formed the majority in the USA. The quota system led to a growing prejudice against immigrants from Southern and Eastern Europe. The greatest prejudice, though, was still reserved for black Americans.

Blacks in southern states not only faced discriminatory laws such as segregation (separation) from whites on buses, they also faced – together with Jews, Catholics, drunkards, divorced people, or anyone who did not fit the WASP ideal – intimidation from a white supremacist group, the Ku Klux Klan. This organisation, first formed in the 1860s, was now revived. The Klan terrorised its victims in a campaign of beatings, castrations, burnings or lynchings, knowing such punishments were all illicit.

397,081	363,599	189,051	175,701	152,792	149,671	131,262	118,647	110,586	103,007
Hungarian	Norwegian	Danish	Greek	French	Finn	Dutch	Swiss	Asian	Romanian

reign-
rn
ople in
e USA

20

Poverty amidst plenty

To escape intimidation, discrimination and poverty, thousands of blacks moved to the northern cities. In the 1920s the black population of both Chicago and New York more than doubled: New York's from 150,000 to 330,000 and Chicago's from 110,000 to 230,000. There they faced further racial hostility and competition for jobs from recent immigrants and poor whites, many farm labourers from rural areas.

Why had the poor whites left the land?

Many farmers failed to prosper during the economic boom. Wheat farmers faced competition from Canada; Europe could not afford to buy their produce; and improved techniques and machinery had resulted in a surplus that no one wanted.

The Republicans, still enjoying a mood of confidence, continued with their policy of laissez-faire, failing to intervene to relieve the poverty and unemployment that millions in both town and country were experiencing. In 1928, indeed after a landslide victory, the Republican President Hoover claimed 'the poor house is vanishing among us'. In March 1929 he pointed out that Americans had more bathtubs, oil furnaces, silk stockings and bank accounts than any other country. But the warning signs were there. Industry, like agriculture, had overproduced. The construction industry had begun to slow down in 1926. By the summer of 1929, car sales were declining and, in June, official figures for output in general showed a decline for the first time in four years. Then, as company profits started to fall, investors began to sell their company shares. Throughout September and October share-selling rapidly gathered pace and on October 29 it accelerated completely out of control.

▲ Children playing in a poor New York suburb

61

Companies need money to pay staff, rent premises, etc.	Raise money from investors	In return, investors own shares in company	Shareholders can receive dividends on share of profits made, or sell shares on Stock Market (Wall Street)	If more people buy than sell, share prices go up; if more people sell than buy, share prices go down

Stock Market investment

BOOM
13
THEN CRASH

The Wall Street Crash

1929

WALL STREET

Radio shares 3.9.1929 ¢505/13.11.1929 ¢28

Anaconda Copper shares 3.9.1929 ¢162/13.11.1929 ¢70

Woolworths shares 3.9.1929 ¢251/13.11.1929 ¢52

General Motors shares 3.9.1929 ¢182/13.11.1929 ¢36

October 23
6m shares sold

October 24
'Black Thursday'

12.9m shares sold

Banks intervene: buy shares to stabilise prices

October 28
9m shares sold

October 29
'Black Tuesday'

Massive fall in share prices

Total panic

Banks do not intervene

16m shares sold

Shareholders lose total of $10m

Share prices, so unrealistic and inflated, no longer reflected true value of companies

Speculators able to 'buy on the margin' borrowed money to buy shares and kept prices high

Banks involved in speculation; $9 billion loaned in 1929

1920: 4 million shareholders
1929: 20 million shareholders

No export market for surplus US goods; Europe could not afford them and had tariffs to protect its own industries

Banks involved in speculation go bust

Rich lose most as more invested

American economy suffered from over-production and falling demand

Warehouses stocked with unsold goods

Mass of people unable to buy share of consumer goods to support level of production

Poor could not even afford hire-purchase schemes to buy goods

Average wages low; higher wages would have meant greater demand for goods

Trade unions weak; not enough pressure on employers to raise wages

Bankruptcies, homelessness, stories of suicides

CRASH

INDIVIDUALS FINANCIALLY RUINED WORLDWIDE

dustrial and farm oduction fell by)%, average ages fell by 60%	625 banks failed. International trade $10 billion.	2,294 banks failed. International trade $3 billion.	International trade $3 billion	By now, over 100,000 businesses had gone bankrupt, 14 million people were unemployed, 5,000 banks had failed
928–1933	1929	1931	1932	1933

The Great Depression

Who lost money in the Wall Street Crash?

Single and major investors, stockbroking firms and banks.

Banks were hit when customers were unable to repay loans made to buy shares, and those banks that had speculated on the Stock Market faced bankruptcy. Losing confidence in the economy, people withdrew their money from banks and did not spend it on goods or shares. As demand for these declined, so did industrial output. Workers were laid off, unemployment soared and the cycle of depression entered a downward spiral, which resulted in what became known as the Great Depression.

By 1933, one in every five adults in the USA was unemployed. Thousands, unable to repay loans and keep up mortgage payments, were evicted from their homes. Makeshift shanty towns, humorously though sarcastically called 'Hoovervilles' after the President, were built. Charities set up soup-and-bread kitchens and 'breadline' queues of unemployed men were a common sight.

Many Americans, who had prided themselves on a pioneering spirit of self-reliance, found the experience of poverty humiliating. President Hoover, nevertheless, continuing the Republican policy of laissez-faire, at first insisted that prosperity was just around the corner.

In 1932 thousands of ex-servicemen marched on Washington to ask for their First World War bonuses (pensions) to be paid early. Hoover sent in armed troops, tanks and tear gas to disperse these Bonus Marchers.

The Republicans did take some steps to relieve unemployment, but by the time of the presidential election of November 1932 these were regarded as being too little, too late. It was the Democrat candidate Franklin D Roosevelt who, pledging a 'New Deal for the American people', swept to victory.

▲ The Great Depression

The first one hundred days

March 4

Inauguration of President Roosevelt. Priorities were:

- relief for the old, sick and unemployed.

- recovery – to get the unemployed back to work.

- reform – to make sure the Great Depression could never happen again.

March 6

Securities Exchange Commission. All banks closed. No gold, silver or coins of any kind to be taken out of USA.

March 9

Emergency Banking Act. Only banks with properly managed accounts and enough cash allowed to reopen (70 per cent did so). Banks' money not to be used in gambling on Stock Market.

March 31

Civilian Conservation Corps (CCC): First 'Alphabet' Agency. Gave work to unmarried men aged between 18 and 25 whose parents were out of work. Run jointly by US Army and US Forestry Service. Work camps set up in America's woods and forests. Men given food, shelter and a dollar a day. Some money to be sent home each month.

- Improved and conserved country's forests.

- Treated tree diseases.

- Restored historical battlefields.

- Made reservoirs, fishponds and fire look-outs.

- 2.5 million men helped by scheme.

May 18

Tennessee Valley Authority (TVA) to deal with problem of farming in the Tennessee Valley.

- Series of dams built on River Tennessee and tributaries.

- These controlled flooding, which swept away topsoil.

- Dams provided electric power and irrigation.

- Electricity used to make cheap fertiliser.

- More crops grown, soil erosion prevented.

- Huge forests planted to stop further soil erosion.

- 1000km of river opened to shipping.

- Created thousands of jobs.

- Regarded as 'flagship' of the New Deal.

phabet encies: sis of w Deal	New Deal for unemployed: FERA, PWA	Temporary work for 4 million: Civil Works Administration (CWA)	New Deal for farmers: AAA	New Deal for land: TVA, CCC	New Deal for industry: NRA	

33   November   NRA symbol

'Action and action now'

March 12

Roosevelt's first radio 'fireside chat' to encourage Americans to put money back into banks. Many did, and crisis passed.

▲ President Roosevelt

March 15

Economy Act. Cut pay of everyone working in government and armed forces by 15 per cent. Cut budgets of government departments by 25 per cent.

March 20

Beer Act. Manufacture and sale of beer made legal again. First step towards ending Prohibition. Money was raised from tax.

May 12

Agricultural Adjustment Administration Act (AAA). Subsidies to farmers in return for producing fewer crops and less food to prevent overproduction. In 1933, 10 million acres of cotton were destroyed and 6 million pigs were slaughtered to raise prices.

May 12

Federal Emergency Relief Administration (FERA). Gave money to states to help them provide relief for the poor. $500 million spent on soup kitchens, blankets, nursery schools and employment schemes.

June 13

Home Owners Loan Company (HOLC). Loaned money at low interest rates to help home owners keep up mortgage payments. 300,000 loans made within a year.

June 16

National Insurance Recovery Act (NIRA). Part 1: Public Work Administration (PWA) provided short-term employment for millions in building of schools, roads, bridges, airports and dams. Part 2: National Recovery Administration (NRA) banned child labour and improved working conditions. Voluntary membership (over 2 million individuals joined). Workers allowed to join trade unions. Encouraged fair competition by setting limits on production and prices charged.

The first New Deal

Was the New Deal considered successful?

It lifted the spirits of American people, it gave employment to thousands, and it restored confidence in the government. But Roosevelt soon came under criticism.

A number of ambitious politicians criticised it for not doing enough to solve America's problems. The governor of Louisiana, Huey Long, wanted greater taxation for the rich, confiscation of all fortunes over $5 million and a 'Share Our Wealth' scheme to give every family $6,000 to spend.

Long was assassinated by opponents in 1935, but other politicians with similar schemes joined forces and attracted much support. Other critics, both Democrat and Republican, were concerned at the expenditure needed to establish the New Deal.

Rich Americans resented paying higher taxes, and businessmen objected to interference in their affairs and Roosevelt's support for trade unions. Others questioned the morality of destroying crops and livestock as ordered under the AAA. Also, the AAA had raised incomes of farmers but not those of the 'sharecroppers'. These were small farmers, mostly blacks, who had to give up a share of their crops to their landlords. Once crops were destroyed and livestock slaughtered, they had no work and were forced to leave their shacks to look elsewhere for work.

Roosevelt also faced, early in his presidency, an agricultural crisis in the mid-West states. Years of overfarming there had exhausted the soil and hot summers had turned the land into a huge 'dustbowl' of loose, dry earth. When autumn winds blew, the earth was whipped up into dust storms that buried cars and buildings, thus forming dust dunes. In 1936 a Resettlement Agency was set up to help these ruined farmers. Most by then, however, had migrated to California to seek work.

▲ A 'dustbowl' farm in Oklahoma

| A replaced National our lations Act agner Act) | The right to join and form trade unions | AAA replaced by Soil Conservation Act, which gave money to farmers who improved soil | Works Progress Administration (WPA): work schemes for photographers, artists and researchers | Social Security Act provided pensions, unemployment insurance, and help for the disabled and children in need |

35

The second New Deal

▲ The landslide victory of 1936

In 1935 the nine judges of the Supreme Court, who were mostly Republicans, declared the NRA and AAA unconstitutional. They ruled that the federal (national) government was responsible for national affairs affecting all states, but, in matters such as helping farmers, individual state governments were responsible.

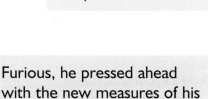

How did Roosevelt respond?

Furious, he pressed ahead with the new measures of his *second* New Deal, quickly replacing the NRA and AAA.

A National Labour Relations Act stated that employers must allow unions in their industries. The Works Progress Administration (WPA) took over all organisations responsible for creating work and provided more employment schemes. A Social Security Act set up pension schemes and unemployment benefits for the first time. In 1936 President Roosevelt made the second New Deal the central issue of the presidential election campaign. He was returned in the greatest landslide victory for more than a century. At this point, however, Roosevelt made a serious misjudgement.

To create a Democrat majority to help pass his measures, he asked Congress to give him powers to appoint six new Supreme Court judges. Protests from both Republicans and Democrats, who feared he was over-reaching the powers granted to a president, forced him to back down.

Despite all the New Deal initiatives, meanwhile, unemployment remained stubbornly high. It was to take another world war to return full employment to the USA. The New Deal was nonetheless significant. It was the first time an American government had accepted responsibility for the vulnerable members of society – the poor, the sick and the elderly. Above all, Roosevelt ensured that democracy survived in America.

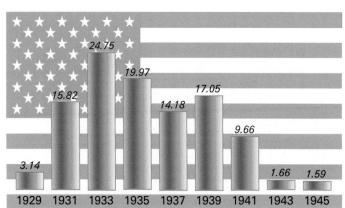

3.14	15.82	24.75	19.97	14.18	17.05	9.66	1.66	1.59
1929	1931	1933	1935	1937	1939	1941	1943	1945

▲ Unemployment as a percentage of the workforce

Russian census estimated population 125 million	A Russians B Finns C Poles	D Ukrainians E Cossacks F Georgians	G Armenians H Uzbeks I Kirghiz	J Kazakhs K Mongols L Tartars	M Yakhuts 55 million Russians, 70 million others of 22 different nationalities

1897 Some peoples of Russia

TSARIST RULE IN RUSSIA

15

The Russian Empire

It would seem – from this map of Europe – that, after the First World War peace treaties had been signed, the Allies had made a Europe safe for democracy. Most countries had democratically elected governments and were early members of the League of Nations.

These countries formed a protective belt against Russia with its revolutionary government hostile to the democracies of the West.

How did a revolution occur in Russia?

There were several long- and short-term factors that made revolution there possible.

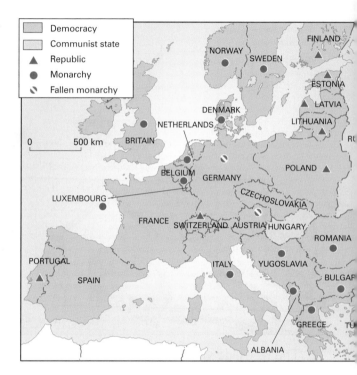

Democracy	
Communist state	
▲	Republic
●	Monarchy
◔	Fallen monarchy

▲ Europe in 1919

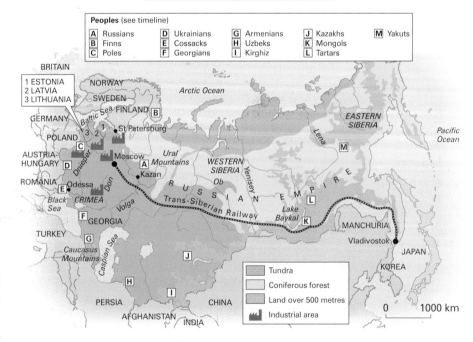

Peoples (see timeline)

A Russians D Ukrainians G Armenians J Kazakhs M Yakuts
B Finns E Cossacks H Uzbeks K Mongols
C Poles F Georgians I Kirghiz L Tartars

Tundra	
Coniferous forest	
Land over 500 metres	
Industrial area	

▲ The Russian Empire in 1900

Russia's size, twice that of the USA and Canada combined, was a factor. Even after the Trans-Siberian railway was completed in 1917, it took 13 days to travel from Moscow in the west to Vladivostok in the east. Travellers undertaking the journey may well have heard several different languages spoken – Russia, after centuries of conquest, had become a land of 22 different nationalities. Only 40 per cent of the population spoke Russian as a first language. This made administration difficult. Furthermore, communication was hampered by long distances, geographical features and climatic extremes. Since the 16th century this vast Russian Empire had been ruled by immeasurably wealthy autocratic Tsars.

omanov ynasty of ars	Peasants released from serfdom (slavery)	Coronation of Tsar Nicholas II	Wife Alexandra of Hesse (granddaughter of Queen Victoria)	80% of population peasants	10% of population nobility and landowners who owned 75% of land
513	1861	1895		1900	

Tsar Nicholas II

What is an autocrat?

Autocrats have complete power to make laws and govern as they wish. Tsar Nicholas II, who was crowned in 1895, believed totally in his divine (i.e. god-given) right to rule.

His word, quite literally, was law. His advisers and top army leaders came from a small number of immensely wealthy families, and it was they and the Romanov family who essentially ruled Russia.

The Tsar's power was maintained with the help of his army, his secret police (Okhrana), and the Russian Orthodox Church, which preached to its congregations that 'God commands us to love and obey every authority and particularly the Tsar'. The bulk of these congregations comprised peasants, who formed 80 per cent of Russia's population. Released from serfdom only in 1861, most were desperately poor, living in village communes (mirs) and working plots of land following the open three-field system with strip-farming. For this land 'given' to them in 1861, they had to make heavy annual payments.

The Tsar, like his father, was keen to modernise and industrialise, and thousands of peasants flocked to the cities – especially the capital at that time, St Petersburg – to find work. Workers, usually young men, faced long hours in often unsafe conditions for low pay. The factory owners, industrialists, bankers and businessmen, on the other hand, had become a new wealthy class of capitalists. If discontent surfaced among the workers, the Okhrana crushed it. Public meetings were controlled, censorship applied, trade unions and political parties banned. Furthermore, there was no elected parliament to represent the workers.

The Tsar began to face opposition from three main parties.

▲ Tsar Nicholas II and Tsarina Alexandra, with their children

Opposition to the Tsar

▲ Primitive society

One group, the Liberals (Kadets), were mostly middle-class professionals who wanted to keep the Tsar but have a democratically elected parliament as well. Another group, the Social Revolutionaries (SRs) were mostly peasants who wanted to overthrow the Tsar and hand over land to the peasants to farm in communes. They were prepared to use violence to further their cause. The third group, the Social Democrats (SDs), wanted to overthrow the Tsar and seize power for themselves. They followed the communist ideas of Karl Marx, a German writer and political thinker.

What is Marxist communism?

Marx believed that each country progresses through several stages of political development until it reaches the perfect stage where everyone lives as an equal in a peaceful communist society.

▲ Feudal society

Progress towards this *perfect* stage, however, is not always peacefully achieved. This is because, according to Marx's theory, history is the story of 'class struggles'. It is necessary, at certain stages in a country's development, he wrote, for the oppressed classes to overthrow the ruling class by means of a revolution. In early primitive societies, where no one owns land and all people are equal, there are no classes. A revolution is not required to move to the next stage. In the second 'feudal society' stage, the nobles who own land are the ruling class. Most people, the peasants, work the land and, as some prosper to become merchants and factory owners, they become the bourgeoise class. These bourgeoise resent the power of the nobles who make laws to protect themselves. To move on to the next stage, a revolution is necessary. The oppressed bourgeoise overthrow the ruling nobles.

Marxist communism

In the third 'capitalist society' stage, the bourgeoise, especially the factory owners, dominate. Most people, the proletariat, work in factories. The proletariat resent the factory owners as they keep the capitalist profits for themselves. To move forward, a revolution is necessary. The oppressed proletariat overthrows the ruling bourgeoise.

In the fourth 'socialist society' stage, the proletariat (the working class) now dominates. It gains control and takes over land and industry, but everyone shares the wealth produced. Gradually people become more equal and the notion of classes disappears. There is no need for a revolution to reach the final 'perfect' stage of communism. Now all are equal, there is enough for all, and it is distributed according to needs.

▲ Capitalist society

Is there a government?

Yes, one does rule on behalf of the people, but, as selfish desires disappear, this government withers away.

▲ Socialist society

In 1903 the SDs split into two groups. The Mensheviks, led by Martov, thought that the Russian proletariat was not yet large enough to stage a revolution. He was prepared to work with other groups to build a larger proletariat. The Bolsheviks, led by Lenin, wanted a small party to carry out a revolution on behalf of the proletariat.

The two groups began to disagree. At the same time, both were illegal and were infiltrated by the Okhrana. Leaders, including Lenin, left to go into exile. Most peasants continued to support the SRs, not the Marxist SDs.

▲ Communist society

Russo–Japanese war	Bloody Sunday	Assassination of Tsar's uncle	First Petrograd Soviet; others set up later	October Manifesto promises a constitutional democracy	All 300 members of Petrograd Soviet arrested
1904–1905	1905 January 22	February 17	October 26	October 30	December

The Revolution of 1905

By 1905 the Tsar's ministers, concerned about economic depression, several strikes and growing opposition from the Kadets, SRs and Marxists, warned Nicholas that a revolution was possible. To regain popularity, the Tsar decided to enter a war with Japan, but a series of humiliating defeats in this conflict fuelled further discontent.

▲ The march towards the Winter Palace in St Petersburg

On Sunday, January 22, 1905 a peaceful demonstration of about 200,000 workers – some holding icons and portraits of the Tsar and led by a priest, Father Gapon – marched to the Tsar's Winter Palace in St Petersburg. Their petition asked for a minimum wage, an 8-hour day and basic civil rights. The Tsar was absent but, without warning, stationed troops opened fire, mounted Cossacks charged, and nearly 200 people were killed. This incident, known as Bloody Sunday, undermined the Tsar's reputation as the 'Little Father of Russia' and led to immediate and widespread unrest in industrial cities. Then, in February, the Tsar's uncle was assassinated. Strikes, burnings and looting of properties, murders of landlords and a naval mutiny were followed in turn by a general strike of 2.5 million people. Workers in cities set up improvised councils (Soviets) that organised strike action and temporarily took over powers of local government.

What did the Tsar do?

In a document called the October Manifesto, he promised the Russian people a Duma (elected parliament), and civil rights and liberties such as freedom of speech. Reassured, people went back to work, but the Tsar's loyal police and army now arrested strike leaders and revolutionary workers. By March 1906 the Revolution was completely crushed.

st World War eaks out	About ¼ of men at front had no weapons	Collection and distribution of food badly managed	Few trains	Fewer men and horses to work land	Shortage of coal for winter	Prices rose almost 700% during war	Murder of Rasputin (by cyanide poisoning, stabbing and drowning)
14 August	1915				1916		December 30

Russia at war

Did the Duma work?

Its powers were very limited, and it soon became clear that the Tsar had no intention of giving up his autocratic rule.

Any progress the Duma was able to make was interrupted by the outbreak of the First World War in 1914. The Tsar at first enjoyed a surge of patriotic support and enthusiasm but, as his army began to suffer heavy defeats against the Germans, and the Russian economy began to disintegrate, this did not last.

In September 1915 the Tsar decided to take personal command of his army and leave his wife Alexandra in charge of the Petrograd government. The Tsar, who was not an able commander, now risked being blamed personally for continuing defeats. The Tsarina, distrusted because of her German birth, was also the subject of widespread rumours about her possible intimacy with a 'holy man' of dubious credentials, Grigory Yefimovich, nicknamed Rasputin (which means 'immoral' or 'corrupt').

Rasputin had gained favour with the royal couple by his seeming ability to heal their only son Alexis of haemophilia, a blood-clotting disease. As his dominance – particularly over the Tsarina – grew, he was able to use his position at court to influence government appointments. Soon, able ministers were replaced by incompetent ones.

On December 30, 1916 a small group of nobles, wanting to save Russia, murdered Rasputin. But by then Russia was in chaos. Soldiers, peasants and workers were suffering terrible hardships. With insufficient raw materials for the factories and shortages of food and fuel for the towns, a wave of strikes began to spread.

▲ The dominant Rasputin – the cartoon reads: 'The Russian Tsars at home'

73

Strikes spread	Provisional Government set up	Petrograd Soviet set up again	Bolsheviks have approximately 10,000 members	Tsar agrees to abdicate	Germans, keen for Lenin to spread ideas of peace, smuggle him out of Switzerland into Russia
1917 January	February 27		March	March 2	April 3

THE RUSSIAN **16** REVOLUTION

The February Revolution, 1917

After a severe winter, food shortages and rising prices, strikes intensified. On February 23, 1917 – International Women's Day – thousands of women joined strikers from the Petrograd steelworks. Numbers out in the streets demanding bread and the removal of the Tsar grew to over 200,000.

Дни революціи.
Войска на Литейномъ просп.

▲ The Cossacks of the Petrograd garrison demonstrating against the Tsar

The Tsar, away from the capital, ordered the Petrograd garrison to help the police put down the revolt. They refused, and in some cases fired on the police. Indeed, most soldiers joined the demonstrators. On February 27 the Duma, too, disobeyed the Tsar's orders by refusing to adjourn. Instead they selected a committee to appoint a Provisional Government of mostly Kadets. This was to be the temporary government of Russia until a permanent one was elected in October. On the same day, Petrograd set up its own 'government': revolutionaries, mostly SRs and Mensheviks, and a few Bolsheviks, formed a Soviet again. This was to speak for the soldiers and workers of *all* Russia.

Faced with this situation, and warned by his army commanders that they could no longer support him, the Tsar decided to abdicate. Within a week, he and his family were arrested and, for their own safety, moved to Siberia.

On March 12 the few Bolsheviks in the Petrograd Soviet were joined by two Central Committee members, Stalin and Kamenev, who had returned from exile in Siberia.

Where was Lenin at this time?

In exile in Switzerland. When he heard that his fellow Bolsheviks were contemplating a reunion with the Mensheviks and were prepared to accept the Provisional Government, he was determined to prevent this.

irth of eon otsky	Exiled to Siberia for organising strike and printing revolutionary literature	Returned for revolution, exiled again	Supported Mensheviks and Provisional Government	Moved over to Bolsheviks, imprisoned in July	On his release, organised Petrograd Soviet
79	1898	1905	1914	1917	

All power to the Bolsheviks

On his arrival in Petrograd on April 3, 1917, Lenin immediately took control of his party. In his April *Thesis* he laid down ten principles to guide the Bolsheviks towards eventual revolution. A main aim was 'no support for the Provisional Government' which, after initial popularity, was losing ground.

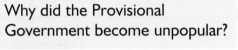

Why did the Provisional Government become unpopular?

▲ Lenin arrives in Petrograd, April 3, 1917

For two main reasons. First, they decided to continue with the ongoing World War, but when an offensive in June against the Austrians failed, morale was seriously weakened and there were mass desertions from the army. Second, they delayed their promised transfer of land from the Tsar, the Church and landowners to the peasants, who now began to seize it for themselves.

▲ Lenin escapes in disguise, July 1917

Lenin, with his slogans of 'Bread, peace, land' and 'All power to the Soviets', took advantage of this mistrust between government and soldiers, workers and peasants, to attract considerable support for his party. But, in July, demonstrations in which the Bolsheviks were involved against the government failed. With some of his colleagues branded as enemies of the state and with members being arrested, Lenin escaped into exile in Finland.

It was an unexpected incident that dramatically revived the fortunes of the Bolsheviks. In August a new commander of the army, General Kornilov, attempted to overthrow the government. The government's leader, Kerensky, was forced to call on Bolshevik paramilitary troops – known as the Red Guard and led by Trotsky – to help him defeat Kornilov. This was successful and Bolshevik popularity was restored. Trotsky was elected leader of the Petrograd Soviet.

Bolsheviks have approximately 200,000 members	Congress of Soviets elects new government; Lenin chairman	Trotsky in charge of foreign affairs	Stalin in charge of non-Russians	Treaty of Brest-Litovsk	Moscow becomes capital	Lenin renames Bolsheviks as Communist Party
1917 October	October 26			**1918** March 3	March 10	March 18

The October Revolution, 1917

Trotsky was also head of the Soviet's newly created Military Revolutionary Committee (MRC), which was responsible for gathering weapons for its own defence. He used the MRC as a front to gather weapons for a Bolshevik revolution.

October	7	Lenin returns secretly to Petrograd.
	10	Lenin persuades majority of Soviet Central Committee to support immediate revolution.
	16–24	Lenin in hiding in Petrograd.
	23	Trotsky reports 15 out of 18 armed units in capital support seizure of power by Bolsheviks.
	24	Kerensky at Provisional Government headquarters in Winter Palace. Sends troops to close down two Bolshevik newspapers. Red Guards prevent this. That evening, Lenin goes to party headquarters at Smolny Institute.
	25	2.00am: Revolutionary troops seize city's strong points: bridges, railway stations, central post office, etc.
		3.30am: Revolutionary ships of Baltic Fleet led by cruiser *Aurora* arrive and train guns on city.
		4.00am: Further buildings, including news agency, captured.
		10.00am: Kerensky escapes to try to contact loyal troops to defeat Bolsheviks. Trotsky and Lenin address the Petrograd Soviet and proclaim end of Provisional Government (though at this stage it is still in place).
		9.40pm: *Aurora* fires blank shot at Winter Palace. Troops desert government.
		11.00pm: Guns at Peter and Paul Fortress fire on Winter Palace.
	26	1.50am: Red Guards storm Winter Palace defended by young cadets and women's unit. Six people die in attack. That evening, Congress of Soviets elect a new government. Lenin is appointed chairman.

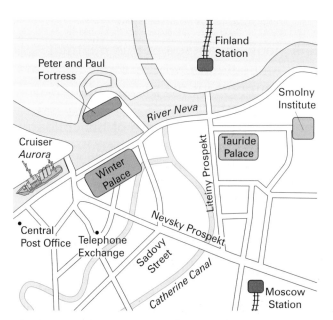

▲ A map of the centre of Petrograd

▲ The storming of the Winter Palace: the reality was rather less dramatic

crees egraphed to all ies, towns and lages	War and Land decrees	8-hour limit on working day; 48-hour week	All non-Bolshevik newspapers banned	Constitutional Democratic Party (Kadets) banned	Cheka (secret police) set up	Factories under workers' control	Banks under Bolshevik control
17 November		December					

Lenín in power

▲ A map of the Brest-Litovsk Treaty, March 1918

Now in power, Lenin acted quickly to keep it. To help deliver his promises of 'Bread, peace, land' he set up a Council of People's Commissars which issued a series of decrees. The first pledged an end to war. The second handed over land owned by the Tsar, the Church and landlords to the peasants. That decree and others which followed aimed to strengthen the Bolsheviks' hold on power. Lenin had also promised free elections to a new Constituent Assembly, but when, as he had anticipated, the SRs became the biggest party, he sent in the Red Guards to close down the Assembly when it opened in January 1918. From this moment the Congress of Soviets, with its Bolshevik majority, passed Lenin's laws.

Was Lenin working towards dictatorship or communism?

Lenin was realistic. He allowed individual ownership of land as he needed the support of the peasants.

He justified his undemocratic policies as he genuinely believed that in time his ideals of true communism would come into being. The Treaty of Brest-Litovsk, meanwhile, marked the end of the war with Germany, but under its terms the old Russian Empire lost Poland and the Baltic States: these included 32 per cent of its arable land, 26 per cent of its railway system, 33 per cent of its factories, 75 per cent of its coal and iron ore mines and 62 million citizens. In addition, the Soviet government had to pay compensation of three million gold roubles.

Lenin's policies and his acceptance of this humiliating treaty made him many enemies and led to civil war in August 1918. In this conflict, the Bolshevik Reds faced several groups of opponents, known collectively as the Whites.

The Reds (Bolsheviks) versus the Whites (social revolutionaries, Mensheviks, supporters of the Tsar, industrialists and landowners)	Foreign intervention by 14 countries	Former wartime allies sent troops and supplies	Czech prisoners of war
1918–1921 Civil war	Assistance given to Whites		

Civil war, 1918–1921

Among the White Armies were troops from Britain, France and America.

Why?

The Whites, some led by the Tsar's generals, promised to continue war against Germany (still proceeding) if successful.

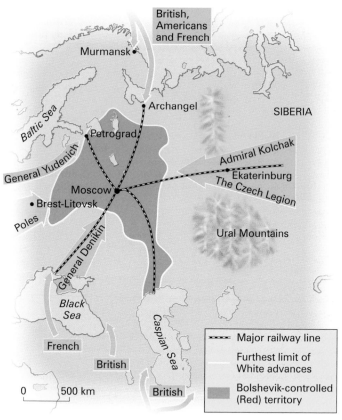

▲ A map illustrating the civil war

At first, against three advancing armies, the Reds were forced into retreat. As White forces approached Ekaterinburg, the decision was taken to execute the Tsar and his family held there. Lenin could not risk the Tsar being rescued and returned as leader of the Whites. Despite appearing to be surrounded (see the map), the Reds had several advantages. They controlled central Russia and its web of railways. This enabled them to keep in touch with their armies and move troops around quickly. The Whites, with fewer men and armaments, were independent units scattered over a huge area, and this made communication among themselves difficult.

The Cheka, in what became known as the Red Terror, made sure that nobody in Bolshevik territories cooperated with the Whites. Even suspected opponents were beaten, hanged or shot. All resources were diverted to the Red Army which Trotsky, as Commander in Chief for War, reorganised. By mid-1920 conscription helped to build an army of 3.5 million men. Discipline was harsh and Trotsky ensured the loyalty of former Tsarist officers by often keeping their families hostage and using loyal party members to watch over those officers. He raised morale by visiting front-line troops. Morale in the White Armies, however – where military strategy was uncoordinated – was low. As these armies attacked separately, Trotsky was able to defeat them one by one. By 1921 the Bolsheviks were in secure control of Russia.

factories taken over by government	Production planned and organised by government	Striking workers risked being shot	Peasants to hand over surplus food to government	Refusers risked being shot	Food rationed	Free enterprise illegal

18–1921 War communism

War communism and the new economic policy

During the civil war of 1918–1921, Lenin introduced emergency economic measures to keep the Red Army supplied with weapons and food, and put communist theories of sharing out wealth among the people into practice.

The peasants, already suffering terrible atrocities at the hands of the White Armies wherever they came into contact with them, also faced cruelties at the hands of the Red Army. Detachments of about 75 men would requisition – forcibly if necessary – all their surplus peasant food. The peasants, who were not paid for producing extra food, refused to grow more. Resulting shortages, combined with drought in 1920 and 1921, led to a devastating famine in which an estimated seven million people died.

In March 1921 a mutiny at Kronstadt naval base took place. Sailors there, resenting increasing party control, wanted civil rights and free elections to be restored in a proper Soviet democracy. The rebellion was crushed but Lenin, aware that the Kronstadt sailors had been among the Bolsheviks' strongest supporters, heeded the warning. That same month he abandoned war communism and announced a new economic policy. To give the peasants greater incentive to grow more food, he allowed them to sell any surplus for profit after paying a tax, and to employ workers. The state kept control of heavy industries, but restored factories with fewer than 20 workers to their original owners to produce small goods.

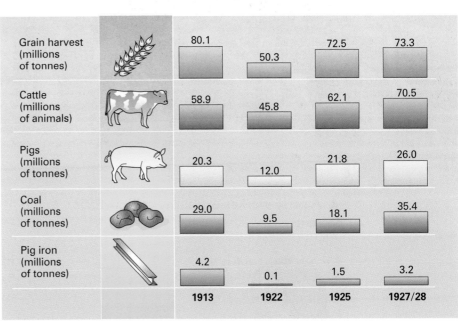

		1913	1922	1925	1927/28
Grain harvest (millions of tonnes)		80.1	50.3	72.5	73.3
Cattle (millions of animals)		58.9	45.8	62.1	70.5
Pigs (millions of tonnes)		20.3	12.0	21.8	26.0
Coal (millions of tonnes)		29.0	9.5	18.1	35.4
Pig iron (millions of tonnes)		4.2	0.1	1.5	3.2

▲ The effects of the new economic policy

But this is not communism!

Lenin was again being realistic. He replied to the critics in his own party: 'Let the peasants have their little bit of capitalism as long as we keep power.'

Cheka replaced by OGPU	Political prisons made permanent	Russian Empire becomes Union of Soviet Socialist Republics (USSR)	Lenin suffers series of strokes	Death of Lenin	Petrograd renamed Leningrad in his honour	No leadership elections
1921		1922	1922–1923	1924 January 21		

Stalin in power

Before his death in 1924, Lenin helped to draw up the constitution that turned the Russian Empire into the Union of Soviet Socialist Republics (USSR). The new leader of the USSR who emerged from the power struggles following Lenin's death was Josef Stalin, the former party secretary.

▲ A party worker explaining collectivisation to the peasants

Stalin, unlike Lenin and other party members who dreamt of eventual worldwide communist revolution, wanted to establish his policy of 'socialism in one country'. He was determined to modernise the USSR so that it could overtake and outstrip the advanced capitalist countries of the West. To industrialise, Stalin needed to raise money to buy new machinery, so he decided to export surplus food. The problem was that Russia was two million tonnes short of grain needed to feed its own people, let alone produce any surplus.

In 1929 Stalin announced that all individual ownership of land would cease. Henceforth peasants were to give up their pieces of land and live on collective farms (kolkhoz) where they would work together for the good of the state.

What were the reasons for doing this?

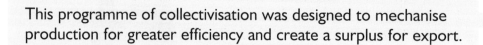

This programme of collectivisation was designed to mechanise production for greater efficiency and create a surplus for export.

Peasants could keep their own homes and a small plot, but carts, implements, horses and livestock would be surrendered to the kolkhoz. An organisation, the Motor Tractor Station (MTS), would provide modern equipment and train the peasants in the way to use it. Ninety per cent of kolkhoz produce was to be sold to the state at a fixed price and the profits shared out. The kolkhoz kept the remaining 10 per cent.

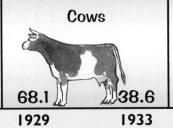  
Collectivisation and dekulakisation

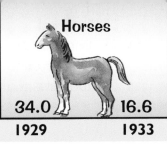

Around 25,000 trained party workers were sent out to encourage the peasants to join the collectives.

Did the peasants want to join?

The poorest who owned no land had nothing to lose, but there was massive opposition from the richer peasants, known as the Kulaks, who each farmed about 10 to 16 hectares.

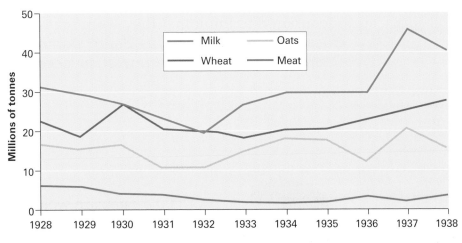

▲ Agricultural output, 1928–1938

They simply refused to hand over their land and produce to the kolkhoz. In 1929 Stalin made his intentions clear: 'We must smash the Kulaks. We must wipe them out as a class.'

Some were shot or imprisoned and their land confiscated. Others were deported to labour camps and the rest were evicted and given inferior land on which to settle. In revenge, many families slaughtered and ate their livestock, smashed tools and burnt crops before surrendering their land.

This 'dekulakisation' programme wiped out over five million Kulaks: thus Stalin lost those farmers most capable of adopting to technological change. Ignorance of new techniques, a shortage of tractors to plough, and continuing resistance from many peasants, led to a fall in production and livestock. In 1932 and 1933 bad weather and poor harvests added to these problems, resulting in famine. As peasants starved, they watched communist officials seize the required quota of grain for export. Reports spoke of peasants eating tree bark, horse manure, and even human flesh to survive. Meanwhile, Stalin persisted with collectivisation despite limited economic success. By 1936, 89.6 per cent of peasants were living on the kolkhoz. This revolution in the countryside, in which a way of life followed for centuries was abandoned, is sometimes called the revolution 'from above'.

Five-year plans	Factories open 7 days a week	Workers followed shift system of 6 days a week	Lateness and absences punished by sacking and loss of living-quarters	Life expectancy in labour camps was two years	Internal passports restricted movement	Skilled workers enjoyed greater pay and better pensions
1928	1929				1932	

The five-year plans

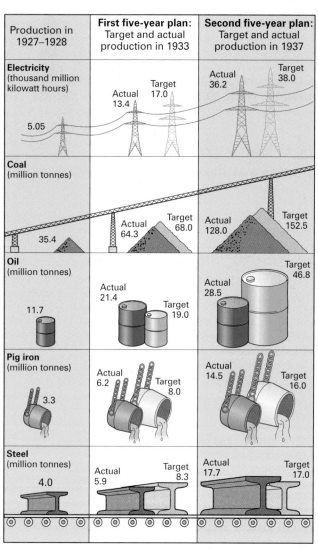

▲ Targets and achievements of the five-year plans

Running parallel to agricultural collectivisation were Stalin's ambitious five-year plans for industry. From 1928, GOSPLAN, the central government agency, set high targets for output and production in major industries such as oil and iron – targets which had to be met every five years. Old industrial areas were redeveloped and expanded and vast new industrial centres were established in the east, safe from possible invasion from the west.

To encourage workers to participate, a propaganda campaign was launched. The people were also encouraged to think that they were taking part in a great crusade for communism, as Stalin wanted to promote the USSR as a beacon of communist success.

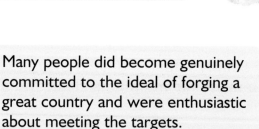

Did the campaign work?

Many people did become genuinely committed to the ideal of forging a great country and were enthusiastic about meeting the targets.

Huge publicity was given to achievements, particularly those of a Ukrainian miner called Alexei Stakhanov, who, in 1935 and with a team of two men, cut 102 tonnes of coal in one six-hour shift, 14 times the average! 'Stakhanovites' became a new élite of workers who received better wages, housing and healthcare. Most workers, though, faced long hours and low wages, which were reduced if targets were not met. Terms of employment were restrictive and criticism of the state risked deportation to forced labour camps (gulags), whose inmates became slave labour on building projects such as canals and railways. Though most targets were not met and the cost in human terms was enormous, achievements were astonishing. Within ten years Russia had the largest power station in Europe, metallurgical complexes, and 'new' industries such as those for machine-tools, synthetic rubber, automobiles and tractors. By 1938 Russia had been transformed into a major industrial power.

rges of mmunist rty	About 1,000,000 out of 2,800,000 purged were party members	1108 out of 1966 party conference delegates purged	93 out of 139 Central Committee members purged	81 out of 103 top generals and admirals purged	7 out of 8 Politburo colleagues purged	Only Stalin left

34–1938

Stalin's purges

For many Russians Stalin provided stability and security. Unemployment was unknown and by the late 1930s workers enjoyed benefits such as training schemes, bonuses for targets met and medical care. Education was free and compulsory. In 1926, 49 per cent of citizens over the age of ten were illiterate. By 1939, this had fallen to 19 per cent. The people, however, never read or heard any adverse comments about Stalin, who was presented in the press and on the radio as a god-like figure.

Didn't Stalin face criticism of his policies?

He did, but from about 1935 he set out to 'purge' (clean out) Soviet society by eliminating his political opponents.

▲ How the purges affected the 'old guard' of 1917

These purges began after the murder of Kirov, leader of the Leningrad communist party. Within 24 hours of his death in December 1934 – which some historians strongly suspect was arranged by Stalin – the death penalty was introduced for all terrorists.

Then the Bolshevik 'old guard' such as Bukharin were purged in 'show trials' in which they confessed to being traitors to the state. Anna Larina, Bukharin's wife, explained his decision to plead guilty: 'He was a child of the party, he was devoted to it.'

Bukharin's loyalty was such that he was prepared to die for the party if required. The party was more important than the individual. The purges went on to affect *all* sections of society, including the armed forces, factories and universities. The reorganised secret police (the NKVD), helped by informers, could arrest and execute people at will. Using a mixture of physical and psychological torture, they were able to extract confessions to any charge they chose to adopt. Few Russians were free from the fear of the knock on the door at night.

Totalitarianism

▲ In this picture taken in St Petersburg in April 1917, the figure of Stalin has been inserted behind Lenin – but Stalin was not actually there

▲ Children were encouraged to join the Young Pioneers, part of the Young Communist League. Members promised 'to love my Soviet motherland passionately and to live, learn and struggle as the great Lenin bade us and the Communist Party teaches us'.

Official cultural policy: music and art carefully monitored to inspire people to follow communism

Citizens bombarded with posters, slogans, radio broadcasts

Manipulation of past: photographs retouched, films re-edited, paintings redone to create myths

Study of Russian language compulsory in all schools

Compulsory lessons in atheism in all schools

Main official textbook written in 1938 by Stalin: *A Short History of the Communist Party*

Army recruits sent where state wanted them to go

Strict censorship: books burned, cardboard pasted over pictures of disgraced communist leaders

Curriculum designed to encourage pride in and loyalty to Soviet Union's achievements

Women's equality promoted but they were often paid less

Communist dictatorship

▲ Josef Stalin, a god-like figure

▲ A communist 'christening' – a party official replaces the priest

Portraits, photographs and statues of Stalin in every town; Stalin Square and Stalin Avenue; processions and poems praising Stalin

One-party state, one leader

Only Communist Party candidates could stand for election to parliament

▲ Communist propaganda: 'Either death to capitalism or under the heel of capitalism'

Monarchy overthrown

Russian Orthodox Church, a rival to 'faith' of communism. Churches destroyed or put to new uses, e.g. as grain stores.

'Supreme Soviet' parliament met for two weeks a year

Show trials: leading Bolsheviks 'persuaded' to confess crimes; executed or deported to labour camps (gulags) in Siberia or Arctic

Millions 'disappeared': doctors, scientists, artists, writers; estimated that 10 million died and 18 million deported to labour camps

Secret police, known as NKVD (formerly the Cheka and OGPU), aided by informers

Totalitarianism: state takes control over lives of individual citizens	Militarism: military values imposed on nation	Fascist right wing opposed to communist left wing	Nationalism: aggressive patriotism love of country

Fascism

19 Fascism

ITALY

▲ The British Union of Fascists with its leader, Sir Oswald Mosley, in 1936

Totally opposed to communism was a new political movement called fascism, which developed in Europe in the second decade of the 20th century.

What does fascism mean?

The word comes from the Latin 'fasces'. These were bundles of wooden rods and axes carried in front of the ancient Roman consuls. The bundles were symbols of the consul's power of life and death over Roman citizens.

This idea, that the state should take control over the lives of citizens (totalitarianism), is an essential feature of fascism, which began in Italy in 1919. The leader of the fascists, Benito Mussolini, wanted to restore the glory of the Roman Empire to Italy by conquering smaller nations. Seeing war as noble and desirable, as fascists do, Mussolini preferred action to discussion and inspired his members with slogans such as:

> A minute on the battlefield is worth a lifetime of peace... Better to live one day like a lion than a hundred years like a sheep... Believe! Obey! Fight!

▲ A fascist parade in Rome

Followers were often ex-army men who had fought in the Great War. The Blackshirts' parades and uniforms were closely modelled on those of the army. Indeed, they wanted to impose military discipline and values on the whole nation. They did not hesitate to use violence to persuade people to vote in their favour. Thus, by 1925, through suppressing the freedom of the press, by closing down 'subversive' organisations, and by searches and arrests, Mussolini had become a virtual dictator. As leader, the 'Duce' (as he was known) inspired almost religious devotion and unquestioning obedience from his followers.

Dictatorships

Did fascism spread to other countries?

By 1939 many right-wing dictatorships modelled on Mussolini's style and tactics had been established in Europe, though they varied enormously in the fascist principles they adopted.

Some dictators failed to attract enough support to create a one-party state as in Italy. In Britain, the Union of Fascists was formed in 1932 under Sir Oswald Mosley. A uniform of black shirts was adopted and there were parades and mass meetings. At first it attracted backing from prominent individuals such as Lord Rothermere, owner of several newspapers. It was, however, the use of increasingly violent tactics by the Blackshirts (as they became known) and their growing anti-semitism (hatred and persecution of Jews) that alienated public opinion and led to Rothermere's withdrawal of support. Clashes between fascists and anti-fascists, communists and Jews, grew.

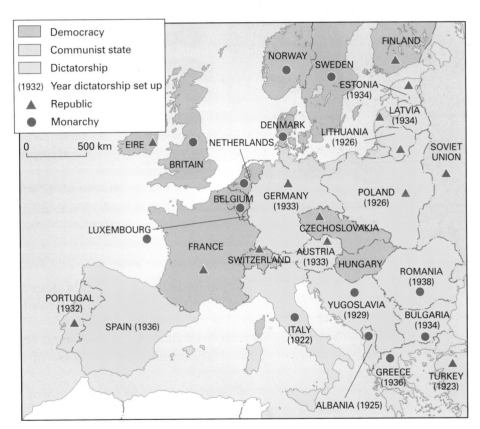

▲ A map of Europe in 1939

On Sunday October 4, 1936, during a march through the East End of London, Mosley and 3,000 Blackshirts were faced with an estimated crowd of 100,000. The resulting fighting, known as the Cable Street Riots, led directly to a Public Order Act that gave the police the powers to ban processions and prohibit the use of uniforms. After that, the BUF fared badly in local elections and the movement in Britain declined.

In Spain, Greece and Turkey the right-wing leaders followed fascist principles with enthusiasm, but it was in Germany and Italy where fascism took hold most strongly.

Towards totalitarianism

▲ A picture from the *Balilla* magazine, published in 1931

'Dopolavoro' offered social welfare, rest and recreational facilities for workers. Organised sporting activities, film shows, subsidised holidays and cheap rail travel.

Flags, celebrations, costumes

Emphasis on spectacle

Rallies and parades

Anti-fascist newspapers closed down and foreign newspapers banned. Censorship of the press.

Radio emphasis on fascist values, e.g. order, obedience and nationalism

Foreign broadcasting available

All cinemas had to show weekly documentary or newsreel about fascism's achievements

Fascist textbooks had to be used from 1930. Nationalistic and military in content.

Teachers had to wear uniform. Rigid control of teachers and curriculum.

Ministry for Press and Propaganda had overall control of radio, cinema, theatre and tourism

Trade unions abolished and strikes forbidden

Women subservient to men. 'Wife and mother' image promoted.

Children from 6 years encouraged to join the Balilla, part of the Fascist Youth Movement. Compulsory membership from 1937. Parades, PE and uniforms were part of the movement. Oath of Allegiance: 'I believe in the genius of Mussolini, in our holy father fascism and in the rebirth of the Roman Empire.'

Fascist dictatorship in Italy

▲ Benito Mussolini

Mussolini – good orator, usually in uniform, hated discussion

Jews not harassed until 1939. Then, Jews prevented from teaching and owning land or large businesses. Not allowed to marry non-Jews or join Fascist Party.

Roman Catholicism became official religion of Italy. Pope supported Mussolini.

Cult of Il Duce (meaning 'the leader'). Portrayed as 'Man of the People'. No mention of his birthdays, illnesses or the fact that he became a grandfather.

One-party state, one leader. Head of State could be removed only by king, not parliament.

Monarchy continued, army loyal to king

All opposition parties banned in 1926

Hatred of communism

About 17,000 people sent to internal exile. Death penalty for political prisoners rare.

Secret police set up in 1926

New court in 1926: special tribunal for political trials

▲ Fascist propaganda: '1919 communism, 1923 fascism'

89

Birth of Adolf Hitler at Branau on Austrian–Bavarian border	Father, customs official, died 1903	Mother, housewife, died 1905	Moved to Vienna	Moved to Munich to avoid conscription to Austrian regiment	Joined German regiment	Awarded Iron Cross First Class	Joined German Workers' Party
1889	1903	1905	1907	1913	1914	1918	1919

GERMANY

20

Adolf Hitler

Hitler, a sincere admirer of Mussolini, became involved in German politics in 1919. He was born in Austria in 1889 and, after school, hoped to study art as a career. Failing to gain a place at college, he spent some time as a 'down and out' before finding a place at a shelter for the destitute. He then made his living by painting and selling scenes of Vienna.

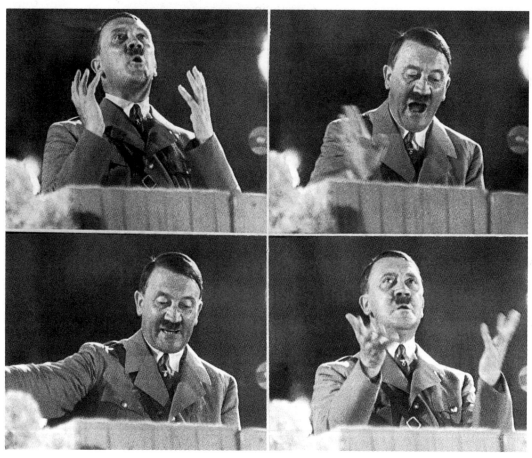

▲ Hitler making a public speech in the 1930s

Moving to Munich in 1913, Hitler was able at the outbreak of war to join a German regiment. Sent to the Western Front, he served with distinction as a regimental runner, earning the Iron Cross in 1918. Hitler enjoyed warfare and was always reluctant to take any leave due. Invalided out after a gas attack, he worked after the war for army intelligence in Munich. Angry at Germany's defeat and the break-up of the German Empire, he decided in 1919 to join the German Workers' Party, one of many right-wing groups at that time.

At his suggestion, the name was changed to Nationalist Socialist German Workers' Party (Nazis) and, by 1921, through force of personality, he had become the 'first chairman with dictatorial powers'.

It was here that Hitler discovered he had a gift for oratory – the art of public speaking. Though his speeches appeared spontaneous and unrehearsed, he spent hours perfecting them, practising gestures and facial expressions in front of a mirror. He could mimic and make his audiences laugh. He won their approval by being able to cope with hecklers. He hung meeting places with banners, and entered to martial music, patriotic songs, dipped flags and a 'Heil Hitler' salute from his private 'army', the SA. He chose a few messages to deliver and repeated them often.

gg cost:	0.9 marks	1.60 marks	7 marks	5,000 marks	4,000,000 marks	320,000,000,000 marks
	1914	1921	1922	1923 July	1923 September	1923 November

The Munich Putsch

What were Hitler's messages?

He attacked the existing democratically elected Weimar government, the Allies, the communists and the Jews for destroying Germany. He appealed to national pride and insisted that Germany could rise again.

In 1923 Hitler decided that the time was ripe for a 'putsch', a revolutionary overthrow of the government. Other right-wing groups at this time had tried to take control of the various German cities as the government and new Chancellor (Prime Minister), Gustav Streseman, were continually being diverted by an economic crisis.

The German economy was in ruins. The country had failed to keep up war reparation payments, and, in 1922, had paid none. In 1923 French and Belgian troops entered the Rühr to seize raw materials and goods owed to them. The government printed money to pay the strikers and pay off debts. As the value of money went down, prices of goods spiralled upwards. More money was printed and this caused hyperinflation. A month's wages were needed to buy a cup of coffee.

On 8 November 1923 Hitler and his supporters launched the putsch. They hijacked a local-government meeting and announced a successful overthrow. Their triumph was shortlived, however. The following day, a march of several thousand Nazis through the centre of Munich was blocked by police. In the resulting mêlée, sixteen SA members and three police officers were killed.

At his trial for treason, Hitler was defiant in defending his views. Sympathetic authorities sentenced him to the minimum five years and well-wishers secured his release in nine months.

▲ Worthless bank notes are destroyed during hyperinflation

The time of struggle

During his time in prison, Hitler wrote the first volume of his book, *Mein Kampf* (My Struggle). In this, he set down his Nazi aims and beliefs.

What were the main ones?

- An end to the Treaty of Versailles.
- A central government led by a single strong Führer (leader).
- Germans were the finest example of the Aryan (white North European) race. All other races, especially the Jews, were inferior.
- The Aryan race would expand through war. War would help Germany gain Lebensraum (living space) at the expense of other nations.

▲ A mass rally at Nuremberg, 1935

Meanwhile, Hitler recognised that power was best achieved within the democratic system. Once in power, he could destroy that system. On his release, though barred from public speaking, he relaunched the Nazi Party. He changed its structure and organisation and made sure that there were plenty of party activists in villages and small towns to spread Nazi ideas.

He surrounded himself with a core of loyal followers and, in 1925, formed the SS, his own personal bodyguard. The military wing, the SA, was prominent at mass rallies, first held in Nuremberg in 1927.

Despite all efforts at drumming up support, however, by 1928, with 13 seats in the Reichstag (parliament), the Nazis were the smallest party. Streseman, who was now Foreign Minister, proved an extremely able politician and was admired both at home and abroad. Democracy seemed safe in Germany.

In 1929 two key events – the death of Streseman and the Wall Street Crash – occurred. Immediately after the Crash, American banks demanded repayment of German loans. German industrial production slumped, businesses went bankrupt and unemployment increased. In such a time of bad economic problems, the people turned to the Nazis who, in 1930, won 107 seats.

ayed radio	Banners, pennants, flags and draperies	Eagle and swastika emblems in strong, bright colours	Motorised cavalcade past thousands of supporters	Torchlight procession, march past in goose-step	12 bands play military marches	Trumpets, drums, chants, speeches, choruses, responses and patriotic songs

ypical mass rally

The rise of the Nazis

Where did the Nazi support come from?

Businessmen, for example, supported *them* rather than the communists, who were also gaining support.

Ex-soldiers supported them because the Nazis wanted rearmament. The middle class voted for them because they thought strong government would prevent hyperinflation like that of 1923. The unemployed backed them because they felt the Nazis would provide work programmes. Helped by his Minister for Propaganda, Joseph Goebbels, Hitler used any technology available – aeroplanes, cars, radios, films or printing – to reach the masses. At the 1929 Nuremberg Rally, 200,000 members and sympathisers were brought in by train. Sixty thousand SA men paraded for three and a half hours in front of Hitler.

In March 1932 Hitler ran for President and polled 13 million to the then President Hindenburg's 19 million votes. After the 1932 July election, the Nazis, with 230 out of 608 seats, became the largest single party, but not a majority one. Although Hitler demanded to be Chancellor, Hindenburg refused. Von Papen continued in that post but had virtually no support. After the 1932 November election, the Nazis lost 34 seats but remained the largest party. Hindenburg again refused to support Hitler as Chancellor. Then, Von Schleicher, the President's adviser and friend, who *had* been appointed, was forced to resign. On January 30, 1933 Hindenburg and Von Papen then offered the post of Chancellor to Hitler.

▲ The Nazis celebrate Hitler's appointment as Chancellor

Why?

They hoped to use the support of the Nazis to help themselves stay in power. At the same time, they were confident that they could control Hitler.

93

Hitler becomes Chancellor	Reichstag burns down	State of Emergency	Nazis win 44% of votes	Nazis become majority party	Enabling Act passed: 444 to 94 votes	Trade unions abolished	Opposition parties banned
1933 January	February 27	February 28	March		March 23	May 2	July 14

From Chancellor to Dictator

As soon as he became Chancellor in January 1933, Hitler called for another election.

▲ The Reichstag in flames, February 27, 1933

Why?

Until the Nazis became the *majority* party, he could not eliminate the opposition.

Fifty thousand SA and SS men were drafted into the police. They broke up communist meetings and arrested leaders and supporters of opposition parties. Then, on February 27 in a dramatic turn of events, the Reichstag building mysteriously caught alight.

A young Dutch ex-communist, Marius von Lubbe, caught in the act of starting the fire, was arrested. Although he insisted he was acting alone, the Nazis immediately claimed this had been a communist-inspired action. Wasting no time, the Nazis arrested as many as 4,000 communists and the next day Hitler persuaded Hindenburg to declare a State of Emergency. This provided the Nazis with a 'legal' warrant to imprison without trial. A further estimated 25,000 Nazi opponents were arrested. As many Germans took this threat of a communist challenge seriously, Hitler's drastic actions were widely accepted and his popularity received a welcome boost.

The campaign propaganda was intensified. In the March election, 44 per cent of the electorate voted for the Nazis. When the smaller Nationalist Party decided to join them, the Nazis gained majority control of the Reichstag. But Hitler wanted complete control of Germany. He introduced an Enabling Act which would allow him to make laws for four years without consulting the Reichstag. To make sure it was passed, communists, under the emergency powers, were banned from taking their seats. Members of the Social Democratic Party were threatened and attacked by the SA when they turned up to vote. Many did not turn up at all. The Enabling Act was passed. Germany was now a one-party state in the hands of a dictator.

A (Sturm -teilung): torm oopers', rownshirts'	SA under Röhm	SS (Schutzstaffel): élite protection squad within SA, 'Blackshirts'	SS under Himmler	First concentration camp opened at Oranienburg	Night of the Long Knives	Police merged with SS	Gestapo (Geheime Staatspolizei): secret state police under Heydrich
21	1925	1929		1933 March 21	1934 June 29	1936	

The Night of the Long Knives

Hitler wasted no time in securing his position. Opposition parties and trade unions were banned. Local government and local police came under Nazi control. Hitler felt insecure, however, about the position of the SA, which had about four million members. The public found them arrogant and coarse. The army commanders suspected that the SA leader, Ernst Röhm, wanted it to become a second army, perhaps even replacing the German army itself.

As Hitler tried to limit the SA's military functions, Röhm began to collect additional supplies of arms from abroad and carry out a series of parades and demonstrations. Hitler could tolerate no possible rivals for power.

On the night of June 29, 1934, squads of SS men moved against the SA. Hitler personally arrested Röhm, one of his oldest comrades. Over the weekend, Röhm, and perhaps as many as 400 others, were executed and thousands of others arrested. This became known as the Night of the Long Knives.

▲ Hitler, Goering (right) and Röhm (centre) shortly before his death

The army said it was well satisfied. Many of the German public admired the forcefulness of Hitler's actions. When Hindenburg died shortly after, the office of President was transferred to Hitler without delay. He dropped the title 'President' and created a new one, 'Führer of the German Reich and German people'. Officers, soldiers, civil servants and ministers all had to swear 'before God' a personal oath of loyalty to Hitler. The SS were completely loyal. In 1934 one branch became responsible for the concentration camps. It was here that political prisoners – communists, socialists, trade unionists and churchmen – were held without trial.

'Undesirables' such as prostitutes and beggars sent to camps	300,000 men and women compulsorily sterilised in families with hereditary illnesses	Nuremberg Laws passed	5 out of 6 gypsies killed by Nazis	720,000 mentally ill gassed; public outcry halts programme	5,000 mentally handicapped babies and children killed
1933–1945	1934–1945	1935	By 1939	1939–1941	1939–1945

Minorities and Jews

▲ SA and SS men outside a Jewish shop: 'Germans! Defend yourselves! Do not buy from Jews!'

▲ A marriage between an Aryan woman and a Jewish man results in public humiliation

Not only political prisoners were held in concentration camps. Hitler wanted the racial purity of German people's blood and culture to be protected by the ruthless elimination of social 'undesirables' such as alcoholics, homosexuals, 'sub-human' species such as Slavs, and the mentally and physically handicapped.

Some people entered the camps, others were eliminated in various ways. Those with hereditary diseases were compulsorily sterilised. By 1939 five out of every six gypsies living in Germany had been killed. A programme involving starvation and the giving of lethal injections to mentally handicapped babies and children was begun in 1939, and the mentally ill were gassed.

Hitler regarded the worst contamination of German blood to be from the Jews. He was obsessed with anti-semitism. To him, the Jews, with no country of their own, were like parasites, sucking the wealth from other people and dominating them. In 1933 mass harassment began. A boycott of Jewish shops and businesses was ordered. Jews were dismissed from important posts in the civil service, medical profession and the media. In 1935 the Reich Citizenship Law meant that Jews were no longer protected by the law. They could no longer vote. The Nuremberg Laws passed at the same time banned marriage or sexual relations outside marriage between Germans and Jews. To help prevent physical contact, a police decree of late November 1938 barred Jews from public places such as theatres, museums, sports grounds and swimming-pools. Notices such as 'Bathing prohibited to dogs and Jews' appeared, and park benches were marked 'For Aryans only'.

00 synagogues rned down	7,500 Jewish shops and businesses looted and destroyed	91 Jews murdered	26,000 Jewish men sent to Dachau, Buchenwald and Sachsenhausen concentration camps

38 9 November

Kristallnacht

On November 3, 1938 Herschel Grynszpan, a young Polish Jew living in Paris, received a postcard from his sister informing him that his family had been deported from Hanover to Poland.

Why had they been expelled from Germany?

The Polish government was about to cancel the passports of all Jews who had been out of Poland for five years or more. The Germans quickly rounded up 15,000 Polish Jews and returned them.

▲ A cartoon from the Nazi newspaper, *Der Stürmer*, published in 1935. Jewish shopkeepers were constantly targeted.

On November 7, to avenge his family's mistreatment, Grynszpan entered the German embassy in Paris and shot a diplomat named vom Rath. When vom Rath died on November 9, the Jews in Germany anticipated some sort of reprisal. That night, the SA and SS – on pre-arranged orders and wielding truncheons, iron bars and clubs – fell on the Jewish community. Synagogues were desecrated and burned, while fireman were instructed to hose down nearby houses to protect *them*. In Jewish districts telegraph lines were cut and electricity and heating cut off. Residents in old people's homes and hospitals were terrorised. Tonnes of shattered glass in the street gave November 9 the name of Kristallnacht (Crystal Night).

Around 26,000 Jewish men aged between 16 and 80 were arrested and sent to concentration camps. The SS guards were trained to be brutal and some deaths from beatings and shootings occurred. Men were released if they could certify their intention to emigrate without possessions. These mass expulsions were successful. In 1939 Ribbentrop, the German Foreign Minister, wrote that 1938 had been a major step towards the solution of the 'Jewish problem'. Other solutions were yet to be decided.

Daily timetable at a girls' school	German	Geography, history, singing (alternately)	Race studies and ideology	Break, sports, science, announcements	Domestic science, maths (alternately)	Eugenics, health, biology (alternately)	Sport	Sex education ideology, domestic science (alternately)
	8am	8.50am	9.40am	10.25am	11.00am	12.10pm	1–6pm	Evenings

Education in Germany

Hitler in *Mein Kampf* wrote: 'The crown of the state's entire work of education and training must be to burn the racial sense and racial feeling into the heart and brain of every youth. No boy and no girl must leave school without understanding the necessity and essence of blood purity.'

How did the Nazis achieve this?

Children received racial instruction from the age of six. They were taught to recognise Jews at a glance. An assignment might be to observe a Jew – his way of walking, his bearing, his gestures and movements when talking – and answer the question: 'What strikes you about the way a Jew talks and sings?'

▲ An illustration from a school textbook published in 1935, encouraging Aryans to bully Jews

Textbooks were rewritten. A new subject, eugenics (the scientific study of how to improve races), was introduced. Hitler also wanted the young to have an unshakeable pride in German military history, myths and heroes. *Mein Kampf* became the main history textbook. Young readers read stories that told of the kindness of the Führer. A popular story encouraged children to be as tough as an oak tree in storms and never to back out of a battle – 'Fight! Struggle!' Another told readers to be slim and slender, quick like a greyhound, tough like leather and hard like steel. All subjects had to concentrate on military matters. Chemistry included lessons on chemical warfare. Mathematics lessons taught children about artillery and ballistics. PE and sport were emphasised. The Nazis wanted healthy young mothers and fit soldiers to ensure the continuity of their 'master race'.

npf (Little [arr]ows): hiking, [cam]ping, [lear]ning Hitler's [ide]as	Deutsch Jungvolk (German Young People): oath of loyalty to Hitler, military discipline	Jungmädel (Young Maidens): health-matters and motherhood	Hitler Jugend (Hitler Youth): uniform, military-type exercise	Deutscher Bund Mädel (League of German Maidens): emphasis on preparation for motherhood
[Ag]es 6–10 Boys	Ages 10–14 Boys	Girls	Ages 14–18 Boys	Girls

Hitler Youth

The Nazis aimed to secure total loyalty from young people, so encouraged them to join their youth organisations. By the end of 1933, all other youth clubs, apart from Catholic ones, had been banned or merged with Hitler Youth. By that time, 47 per cent of boys aged between 10 and 14 belonged to the German Young People, and 38 per cent of boys aged between 14 and 18 were members of Hitler Youth. The Hitler Youth Law of 1936 called for all German youngsters to join, and, in 1939, membership became compulsory.

▲ Hitler meets a group of Young Maidens wearing traditional costume. It was considered not proper to wear trousers or too much make-up.

What did boys do?

They went on organised hikes, and stayed at youth hostels and camps. There were sports such as cross-country running and competitions.

They learnt to read maps, and clean and use rifles. There were military-style drills and parades with bands. They might be reminded that the drummer-boys of years ago marched into battle ignoring the wounds they had received and drumming until they fell and died.

There were discussions about political writings, and discipline and obedience to the group were emphasised.

In 1933 girls were less organised. Only 15 per cent of 10- to 14-year-olds and 8 per cent of 15-year-olds belonged to the girls' equivalent organisations. The League of German Maidens focused on good health and housekeeping skills in keeping with Hitler's view of women as wives and mothers. He did not consider it correct that women should become involved in the world of men. The Nazis promoted motherhood and home-making, particularly when the birth-rate began to fall alarmingly.

Typical day at a labour camp	Rise, exercises, washing, bed-making, breakfast	Flag parade, speech by camp leader	March to do farm work	Lunch, rest	Sport	Political lessons	Jobs allocated for next day	Supper	Songs, dancing, speeches	Lights out
Ages 18–25	6–7am	7–7.30am	7.30am–2.30pm	2.30–4pm	4–5pm	5–6pm	6–7pm	7–8pm	8–9pm	10pm

Adulthood in Nazi Germany

Didn't women have careers?

No, in fact discrimination against them was actively encouraged. They were excluded from the armed forces, the government and the practice of law. Politically-minded women were disapproved of and professional women were forced to give up work to look after their families.

▲ A 'Gold Cross' mother

The role of a woman was seen as guardian of the family, mother to her children and obedient helpmate to her husband. Posters, radio broadcasts and newsreels all celebrated motherhood and home-making. Hitler offered tax incentives for married couples to have children. In 1938 the Honour Cross of the German Mother was established to reward fertile mothers. The highest award, the Gold Cross, was given to those with eight children.

Only women who passed tests designed to prove they were biologically and politically suited were allowed to marry members of the SS, the racial élite. Youths were chosen to apply for the SS at the age of 18, but during their training they had to complete, alongside all other men and women of a similar age, six months' National Labour Service. They lived at camps, wore uniforms, were paid pocket money and did manual work such as planting forests and digging ditches.

After that, all salaried workers had to belong to the German Labour Front (DAF), which replaced trade unions. They were not allowed to strike or bargain for higher wages. There was no limit on the number of hours worked each week and employees could not leave a job without permission from the DAF. All these organisations – the schools, youth clubs, camps and Labour Front – led to mass control over the lives of German people.

nemployment Germany	8.4%	13.1%	15.3%	23.3%	30.1%	26.3%	14.9%	11.6%	8.3%	4.6%	2.1%
	1928	1929	1930	1931	1932	1933	1934	1935	1936	1937	1938

'Bread and work'

What happened to workers who protested about working conditions?

Hitler knew that the threats of the Gestapo and concentration camps were sufficient deterrents to troublesome workers.

For many workers, however, Hitler offered stability and security for the first time in several years. The Nazis kept their election promises of 'bread and work' and, between January 1933 and July 1935, over five million jobs were created. The DAF organisation itself provided work as it owned banks and insurance companies. It owned a car plant where a car for the people – the Volkswagen – was built. It controlled the Strength Through Joy (Kraft Durch Freude, or KDF) organisation, which subsidised housing, opened health resorts, helped to pay for holidays and ran coach tours for loyal workers. Temporary manual work was provided by the labour camps.

Public works and conservation programmes were set up. Hospitals, schools, huge buildings such as the Olympic Stadium and a network of autobahns (motorways) were built. More work was created through Hitler's policy of autarky (self-sufficiency). He tried to make Germany less dependent on foreign supplies so that any future blockades might not have such an effect on the economy.

In 1936 a four-year plan was launched, aiming to build up an economy fit for war. More raw materials such as iron and coal were produced and synthetic materials such as plastics and nylon manufactured. Even by 1939, Germany still needed to import over one-third of her raw materials. A rearmament policy creating work for millions, however, had produced an army ready for war by 1939.

▲ A poster for the Strength Through Joy organisation

101

Totalitarianism

▲ A poster encouraging young people to join Hitler Youth. Membership was compulsory from 1939.

▲ Loudspeakers were set up in streets and public bars. Hitler's speeches, and those of other Nazi leaders, were repeated over and over.

Strength Through Joy (Kraft Durch Freude, or KDF) offered mass tourism, subsidised concerts, theatre, sports and other recreational activities for workers

Jazz music banned as it was 'black' music and black people were considered inferior. Work of Jewish composers, e.g. Mendelssohn, banned.

Emphasis on spectacle, mass rallies, parades, processions, flags and martial music

Foreign films censored. All films to carry pro-Nazi message.

All Germany could hear the Führer on the People's Radio – these were short-range sets, unable to pick up foreign stations. Listening to BBC punishable by death.

Textbooks rewritten to reflect Nazi views

No books published without Goebbels' permission. Goebbels controlled Reich Chamber of Culture. Literature, art, music, films, radio, theatre and press all controlled.

Anti-Nazi newspapers closed down

Women subservient to men. 'Wife and mother' promoted.

Trade unions abolished and strikes forbidden

Fascist dictatorship in Germany

▲ Adolf Hitler

▲ Fascist propaganda: 'Victory or Bolshevism (communism)'

Hitler – good orator, usually in uniform, hated discussion

Nazi-dominated Protestant Church. Catholic Church promised to keep out of politics. Nazis did not interfere.

In the 1930s and 1940s Jews were increasingly harassed and persecuted. An estimated six million were killed by the Nazis.

Monarchy overthrown

Cult of der Führer (meaning 'the leader')

One-party state, one leader

All opposition parties banned in 1933

Hatred of communism

Concentration camps later to become extermination camps

'Informers on every staircase'

Secret police

Ordinary police: top jobs to high-ranking Nazis

Control of judges, courts and magistrates

Army oath of loyalty: 'I swear by God that by this sacred oath I will give complete obedience to the Führer Adolf Hitler... and am ready as a brave soldier to risk my life at any time for this oath.'

THE ROAD 21 TO WAR

Rearmament

I thought that rearmament was forbidden by the Treaty of Versailles?

It was, so at first Hitler rearmed secretly under the guise of public works programmes.

In 1933, at the Geneva Disarmament Conference, he claimed he wanted peace and was prepared to disarm if other nations did so. When the other powers could not agree over disarmament, Hitler withdrew from the Conference and the League of Nations. Now he was free to rearm openly.

▲ German troops enter the Rhineland in March 1936

In 1935 a massive military rally celebrated German armed forces. Military spending leapt from 1,953 billion marks in 1934–1935 to 8,273 billion marks in 1937–1938. The necessary uniforms, weapons and equipment set factories, steel mills and coal mines in production and more jobs were created for designers, fitters and engineers.

In 1936 Hitler justified the introduction of conscription by maintaining he was creating a buffer against communism. Many people in Britain and France supported his stance. Hitler knew that Britain felt sympathy towards Germany over the harshness of the Treaty of Versailles. Indeed, Britain had already started to dismantle the Treaty herself. In order to protect her navy, she had allowed Germany to increase *her* navy, but had limited it to 35 per cent of the British navy. The French were furious, but could do little.

Then, in 1936, Hitler took a huge gamble by sending troops into the Rhineland, a demilitarised zone. The League of Nations, occupied with a crisis in Abyssinia (now called Ethiopia), condemned the action but did little else. France, not knowing the strength of the German forces, refused to act without British support, which was not forthcoming. German troops thus remained in the Rhineland.

an leaves	Germany leaves	USSR joins	Italy leaves	USSR leaves	France leaves	Britain leaves
33	1933	1934	1937	1939	1940	1946

The League of Nations

By the 1930s the League's actions were becoming discredited. There had been major disputes in Manchuria, Abyssinia and Spain in which the League had failed to intervene successfully.

Some successes		Some failures

1930

Manchuria Japan attacked the Chinese province of Manchuria. It had rich farmland and raw materials, which the Japanese wanted. When the League ordered them to withdraw, they refused.

1931

Iraq This British mandate became independent. Most other Turkish and German colonies governed by the Mandate Commission became independent after the Second World War.

1932

Japan resigned from the League.

1933

Abyssinia (Ethiopia) Mussolini wanted an empire to make Italy look powerful. Italian troops entered Abyssinia. The League ordered other countries to stop trading with Italy, but oil supplies were continued. When the Emperor of Abyssinia, Haile Selassie, appealed for help, the League did not act. Italy took control.

1934

The Saar This had been controlled by the League since 1919. After a plebiscite (vote), the people voted for this region to be returned to Germany.

1935

1936

Spanish Civil War Fought between communist-leaning supporters of the Republican government and those led by right-wing fascist rebels under General Franco. Stalin helped the communists; Mussolini and Hitler sided with the rebels. Hitler gave his air force (Luftwaffe) experience of war. In 1937 German bombers attacked the Spanish town of Guernica, killing 1,600 people. The League stood by, helpless, while the victor, Franco, took control of Spain.

1937

1938

1939

105

Peace movement and demonstrations	Labour Party: pacifist inclined	Support for disarmament	Anti-war literature, music and paintings	Anti-war authors: Henri Barbusse, Robert Graves, Wilfred Owen, Siegfried Sassoon, Ernest Hemingway	All Quiet on the Western Front written by E M Remarque (German). 2½m sold in 18 months, made into Hollywood film, Nazis burnt this book.

Anti-war gestures in the 1920s and 1930s

Austria

By 1937 Hitler had much to celebrate. The people of the Saar had voted peacefully to join Germany. He had occupied his 'back door', the Rhineland. He had also signed an agreement with two military dictatorships, those of Italy and Japan. Under this Anti-Comintern Pact, the influence of international communism was to be halted. These successes gave Hitler the confidence to proceed with his programme of 'race and space'. If he could unite with Austria and conquer Czechoslovakia, he could extend his frontiers, add manpower to his forces, utilise valuable resources and create one strong nation-state.

The Austrian Nazi Party was ordered to begin a campaign of riots and demonstrations to bring about an Anschluss (union) with Germany. Chancellor Schuschnigg tried to organise a vote so that the Austrian people could vote fairly on the issue. To prevent this happening, Hitler threatened military action. Rather than risk bloodshed, Schuschnigg resigned and Seyss-Inquat, a leading Nazi in charge of the police, invited the Germans in to keep order. This they did, imprisoning over 80,000 opponents of Hitler. On March 14, 1938 Hitler entered Austria in triumph. A vote was held and, under the watchful eye of the Nazis, it was found that 99.75 per cent of the people agreed with the Anschluss.

Why did Britain and France not act to stop Hitler?

Neville Chamberlain, Prime Minister of Britain from 1937, favoured a policy of appeasement, which France supported.

▲ Hitler enters Austria, March 1938

By giving way over *some* disputes, Chamberlain trusted that Hitler's aggressive demands would cease. After the devastation of the Great War, the desire for peace was uppermost in the minds of many. When Hitler was asked by Chamberlain whether he had designs on Czechoslovakia, he replied: 'I give you my word of honour, Czechoslovakia has nothing to fear from the German Reich [Empire].'

ar votes return to rmany	Conscription in Germany	German troops enter Rhineland	Luftwaffe gain experience in Spanish Civil War	Anti-Comintern Pact between Germany, Italy and Japan	German troops enter Austria	German troops enter Sudetenland	Britain prepares for war: trenches, air raid shelters, gas masks, evacuation plans	'Peace for our time'
35	1936		1936–1939	1937	1938 March	October		

Sudetenland and the Munich Conference

Three million German-speakers lived in Czechoslovakia, mostly in the Sudetenland. It was they who gave Hitler the excuse to invade Czechoslovakia. Heinlein, the leader of the Sudeten Nazi Party, was urged to seek more and more concessions from the Czech government, which could not be met. In April 1938 German troops massed on the Czech border. The Czech President, Benes, mobilised his troops but was persuaded by Britain and France – both anxious to avoid war – to make further concessions.

Hitler, who wanted the Sudetenland as part of Germany, encouraged the Sudeten Nazis to riot. Benes crushed these riots. On September 15, Prime Minister Chamberlain met Hitler to discuss his demands. As a result, the Czechs were persuaded by Britain and France to transfer to Germany that part of the Sudetenland where most German-speakers lived.

Then, on September 22, when Chamberlain reported back to Hitler, the Führer unexpectedly demanded the whole of the Sudetenland or threatened war. As Britain and France reluctantly prepared to go to war, Mussolini proposed a last-minute conference at Munich. There, with Czechoslovakia not invited, Britain, France, Italy and Germany agreed that the Sudetenland should go to Germany. The Czechs were forced to agree, Benes resigned, and on October 1, 1938 German troops entered the Sudetenland.

The day after this Munich agreement, Chamberlain signed a separate one with Hitler. The two countries promised to consult over any problems and never to go to war again. Chamberlain returned to London and a hero's welcome.

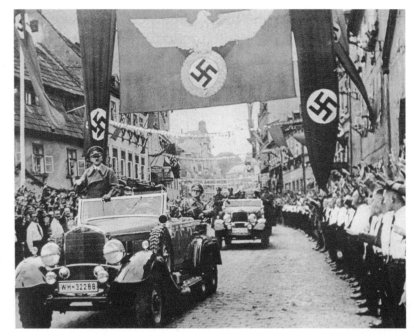

▲ Hitler enters the Sudetenland in October 1938

▲ Chamberlain and 'peace for our time'

The end of appeasement

Once the Sudeten Germans were united with Germany, the Hungarians and Poles living in Czechoslovakia – supported by Hitler – demanded 'independence' too. Soon, both Hungary and Poland took Czech territory. With his country in chaos, the new President, Hacha, offered no resistance when, on March 15, 1939, German troops took over the rest of the country.

▲ A map of Czechoslovakia, 1938–1939

Legend:
- Sudetenland given to Germany at Munich
- October 1938: Teschen taken by Poland
- November 1938 to March 1939: Slovak border areas and Ruthenia taken by Hungary
- March 1939: Remainder of Czechoslovakia taken under German control
- German border in 1939

What did Britain do?

Nothing about *this* situation, but by now parliament and many members of the general public wanted an end to appeasement.

Hitler, confident that Britain and France would not intervene in his next step to gain more Lebensraum (living space) for his 'master race', now turned towards Poland. He demanded the return of the port of Danzig, a former German but now 'free city' in the strip of land known as the Polish Corridor. This land had been given to Poland under the terms of the Treaty of Versailles. The Poles rejected Hitler's demands. Britain, wanting to form a common front against Hitler's aggression, began talks with the Soviet Union. Unknown to the negotiators, however, the Russians were already in secret talks with Hitler.

On August 23, the two 'enemies', fascist Germany and communist Russia, signed the Nazi–Soviet Pact, agreeing not to attack each other. Secretly they decided, in the event of a German invasion of Poland, to divide the country between them. On August 25, Britain signed a formal treaty with Poland committing her to go to Poland's aid if she were attacked by Germany. France entered a similar alliance. Despite all hopes and wishes, however, on September 1, 1939 Hitler ordered his forces into Poland.

...rmany: people moved ...m Saar-Phalz area ...ar the French border	France: about ½ million people moved from the German border to south-west France	City of Benares: liner in convoy from Liverpool to USA and Canada torpedoed. 78 out of 93 children drowned. Sea evacuations ended.
...39		1940 September

Evacuation

Did Britain declare war immediately?

No. Chamberlain and his government still hoped to reach a settlement, but these proposals, once known, were rejected by parliament. The Cabinet demanded war and its unanimous decision for an ultimatum was confirmed.

On September 3, 1939, after a two-hour ultimatum sent to Germany had been ignored, Britain and, later that day, France declared war. Between the first and the third of September, in expectation of German air raids, about two million people moved to safer areas at home and abroad. The government put into action their evacuation plan, Operation Pied Piper. In those three days, almost one and a half million people – mostly children over the age of five, pregnant women, mothers with children under five and the disabled – were evacuated from London and other major cities such as Liverpool and Manchester to the safety of the countryside.

▲ Evacuees from central London arriving at Gravesend, Kent

There they were billeted, and most children housed with foster parents. The children had not been told where they were going or what was going to happen to them. Some immediately loved their 'new' families and their life in the country. Others, after a little homesickness, settled well enough. A significant minority, however, were emotionally scarred by unhappiness or ill-treatment. Carers, unused to real poverty, complained of receiving illiterate and often verminous slum children who spoiled their clean homes. Yet, whilst many children did use face-flannels, toothbrushes and hot water from a tap for the first time, others had to adapt to outside lavatories and homes without electricity. Adjustment depended on the individual personalities of carer and child. As it happened, however, by Christmas, about one in three children had returned home.

Poland: 600,000 Polish soldiers face 1,700,000 German soldiers	Britain and France declare war against Germany	'Phoney' war	Russian troops occupy eastern Poland	Warsaw surrenders unconditionally	Poland partitioned between Germany and Russia
1939 September 1	September 3	September	September 17	September 28	October

Poland

Was it considered safe for children to return?

Yes, as this was the time of the 'phoney' war. War at sea had begun, but there were as yet no military offensives on land in the West.

In the East, Poland, after invasion on September 1, fought bravely against superior German forces while Britain and France hesitated to act. Fighting alongside the regular German army were the SS special units. Their orders were to imprison and wipe out every enemy of Nazism. Enemies included Polish citizens and Polish Jews who were arrested at will, shot at random or killed in reprisals.

From September 17, the secret agreement of the Nazi–Soviet Pact was put into action. Soviet forces occupied eastern Poland prior to partition. On September 28, after a ferocious struggle against a German assault, Warsaw, the capital, surrendered unconditionally. Soldiers who gave themselves up to the Russians rather than the Germans were sent to prisoner-of-war camps deep in the Soviet Union. Thousands of Polish civilians who fled to Russia were sent to labour camps.

The Germans deported more than a million Poles, including prisoners of war, to work in factories and fields as slave labour. The first concentration camps were built in Poland. One, to punish rebellious Poles, was set up near Oswiecim, now called by its German name, Auschwitz.

For the Jews under German rule, another solution was found. They were deported to designated cities such as Lodz and Warsaw and, together with the Jews already living there, were confined to certain districts called ghettos within those cities.

▲ Jewish families in Warsaw being rounded up for confinement in the ghettos

...rmany ...cupies ...nmark	Danish king stays to resist Nazi tyranny	German seaborne attack against Norway	Heavy German naval losses	Norwegian king escapes to Britain and directs resistance from there	Winston Churchill becomes Prime Minister of Britain	Britain withdraws from Norway

40 April 9   May 10   June

Norway and Denmark

By December 1939 Hitler had decided to invade Norway.

Why?

He knew Britain wanted to land troops there to cut off German supplies of Swedish iron ore and establish bases on the coast to strengthen the blockade against Germany.

Hitler wanted the iron ore for obvious industrial uses and coastal bases for his own naval and air offensives against British shipping in the Atlantic.

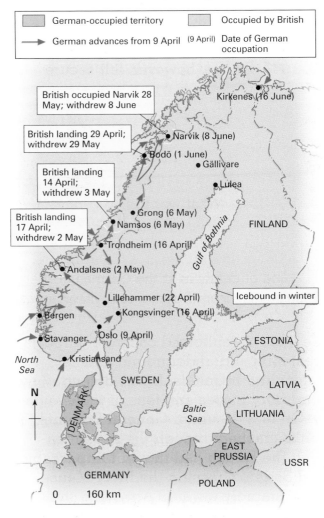

Legend:
- German-occupied territory
- Occupied by British
- German advances from 9 April
- (9 April) Date of German occupation

British occupied Narvik 28 May; withdrew 8 June

British landing 29 April; withdrew 29 May

British landing 14 April; withdrew 3 May

British landing 17 April; withdrew 2 May

Kirkenes (16 June)
Narvik (8 June)
Bodö (1 June)
Gällivare
Luleå
Grong (6 May)
Namsos (6 May)
Trondheim (16 April)
Andalsnes (2 May)
Lillehammer (22 April)
Kongsvinger (16 April)
Bergen
Stavanger
Oslo (9 April)
Kristiansand

FINLAND
Gulf of Bothnia
Icebound in winter
ESTONIA
SWEDEN
LATVIA
Baltic Sea
LITHUANIA
EAST PRUSSIA
USSR
GERMANY
POLAND
DENMARK
North Sea

N

0   160 km

▲ A map showing the German invasion of Norway

On April 9, 1940 German troops entered Denmark and launched a sea attack against Norway. The Danish government refused to declare war and accepted German occupation. Norway resisted, but within weeks the Germans occupied all ports and airfields. Against heavy odds, the British, French and Polish forces opposed the Germans and, in all cases, had to withdraw. After this humiliating failure, Chamberlain lost the support of his government. On May 10 Winston Churchill was appointed Prime Minister of a national government. Churchill had opposed appeasement and favoured rearmament. He had forecast the rise of Nazi Germany and was determined to fight it. He was able, through his stirring speeches, to communicate this determination to the British people. On May 13, in the House of Commons, he declared: 'I have nothing to offer but blood, toil, tears and sweat... You ask, what is our policy? I will say: it is to wage war by sea, land and air, with all our might and with all the strength that God can give us... You ask, what is our aim? I can answer in one word: victory. Victory at all costs; victory in spite of all terror; victory, however long and hard the road may be.'

Blitzkrieg: Luxembourg taken	British Expeditionary Force sent to Belgium	Germans break through Maginot Line	In 3 days, RAF lose half of its 200 bombers in France	French air force destroyed	Holland surrenders, Dutch queen moves to England	Belgium surrenders, Belgian king taken as prisoner of wa
1940 May 10		May 12			May 15	May 28

Luxembourg, Holland and Belgium

By May 13 Hitler was already three days into a fresh offensive – a simultaneous attack against Holland, Belgium, Luxembourg and France. For this he used a new type of mechanical warfare, Blitzkrieg (lightning war), whose key weapons were the radio and the internal combustion engine.

- Bombers 'soften up' the enemy by attacking airfields and industrial centres.
- Parachutists seize key points, e.g. bridges.
- Great columns of light-armoured vehicles – tanks and truck-borne infantry – move into enemy territory supported by air-fighter strikes.
- Fighters scout ahead and on flanks of armoured columns.
- Dive-bombers attack road and rail communications and terrorise civilians.
- Fighter-bombers harass the people in the countryside.

This highly effective warfare, with its emphasis on speed, resulted in the surrender of Holland on May 15 and Belgium on May 28, 1940. France, however, felt secure behind her Maginot Line.

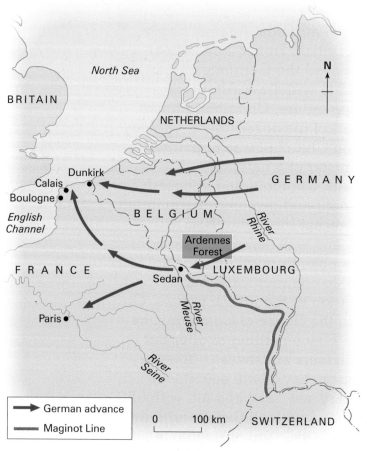

▲ A map of the German invasion of France, May 1940

What was this?

A line of defences at the German border stretching from Belgium to Switzerland.

It had three lines of reinforced concrete outposts, blockhouses, forts and underground arsenals, living-quarters and hospitals. It was defended by enormous artillery pieces and tens of thousands of infantry. On May 12 under General Rommel, German tanks crashed through the Ardennes Forest, which the French had thought impassable, and reached Sedan. Crossing the River Meuse, they advanced rapidly towards Arras and the Channel coast to trap the Allied forces in Belgium. On May 19, when it became clear that the BEF could be cut off, preparations were made to evacuate the Allies from coastal ports. Fortunately for the Allies, however, on May 24 Hitler ordered his troops to halt their advance.

,000 British diers killed taken soner	Left behind at Dunkirk for German use	475 tanks, 400 anti-tank guns	20,500 motorcycles, 64,000 other vehicles	8,000 Bren guns, 90,000 rifles	7,000 tonnes of ammunition	77,000 tonnes of supplies	165,000 tonnes of petrol

40 May 26 to June 4

Dunkirk and the fall of France

On May 24 Hitler issued a directive: 'The next objective of our operation is to annihilate the French, British and Belgian forces, which are surrounded.'

The evacuation of Allied forces began that day. As Boulogne and Calais were taken by the Germans on May 26, the British plan, Operation Dynamo, became focused on Dunkirk. On May 27 Royal Navy destroyers – aided by an armada of 860 other vessels, including pleasure steamers, fishing boats and even yachts – left ports on the English south coast to mount the rescue. The Germans, to prevent such an evacuation, engaged in a

▲ The evacuation of Dunkirk

ferocious air battle with the RAF above Dunkirk. In nine days, 176 German and 106 British aircraft were shot down. Despite fears of heavy military losses, by June 4, 225,000 British and 140,000 French troops had been brought safely across to England. King George VI, in a message to his forces, hailed Dunkirk as a triumph.

Was it?
is

The rescue was a triumph of organisation and many men *were* saved, but Churchill was well aware that wars are not won by evacuation.

The French, now heavily outnumbered in the struggle to the north of their capital, at first defended stoutly. But, as the Germans broke through behind their lines, the entire army began to retreat. On June 14 Paris fell, and on June 22 the French, losing the will to fight, accepted an armistice on German terms. Germany took control of the west coast down to Spain and the northern regions, known as Occupied France. Land south of the River Loire was unoccupied. Here, a 'puppet' government under Prime Minister Marshal Pétain was installed. Vichy, a spa town, became the 'capital'. Hitler was jubilant. He was now master of Poland, Denmark, Norway, Luxembourg, Holland, Belgium and France. But not, as yet, of Britain.

Heinkel He 111 and H and P series: medium-range bombers	Dornier Do17Z (Flying Pencil): medium-range reconnaissance bomber	Junkers Ju87B and Ju88A: dive-bombers	Messerschmitt ME-109 (single engine, maximum speed 570kph) and ME-110 (twin engine, maximum speed 600kph): fighters to protect bombers

Luftwaffe aircraft

The battle for Britain

▲ A Messerschmitt ME-110

Hitler assumed that once France fell Britain would seek peace. Churchill defiantly turned down German approaches for negotiated peace terms. He had already anticipated the possibility of an invasion: 'We shall fight on the beaches, we shall fight on the landing grounds, we shall fight in the fields and in the streets, we shall fight in the hills; we shall *never* surrender.'

What support did Britain have?

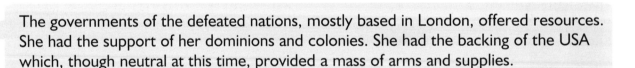

The governments of the defeated nations, mostly based in London, offered resources. She had the support of her dominions and colonies. She had the backing of the USA which, though neutral at this time, provided a mass of arms and supplies.

In July 1940 Hitler decided on an invasion. The plan was first to implement Operation Eagle, an air offensive which, it was hoped, would bomb Britain into submission. Even if this was not achieved, her defences – particularly the fighter squadrons – would be destroyed. Operation Sea Lion could then follow: the German army, escorted by her navy, would land in places between Folkestone and Brighton. The invasion date was, in fact, fixed for September 15.

As the Luftwaffe assembled, Britain prepared. The membership of the Local Defence Volunteer Force (later called the Home Guard), which had been formed in May 1940, soon reached the million mark. Children were evacuated again. Beaches were protected with barbed wire and landmines, and open fields were set with obstacles. Signposts were removed from roads and railway stations. Church bells were silenced – to ring only if the enemy landed. An appeal went out for aluminium coathangers, cigarette boxes and pots and pans to help build aircraft. Senior commanders of both sides knew that success depended on their air forces.

stol Blenheim: ht interception nber	Boulton Paul Defiant: nocturnal missions fighter	Spitfire (maximum speed 600kph): fighter to deal with enemy escorting fighters	Hurricane (maximum speed 550kph): intercepted bomber formations

aircraft

Luftwaffe versus RAF

What was the strength of the Luftwaffe?

In July 1940 Airfleets 2, 3 and 5 had a front-line joint strength of around 3,000 aircraft, of which about 2,500 were ready for action.

Its reserves of planes were few, but they had the best-trained and most experienced pilots in the world. The morale of the Luftwaffe was high. Goering, however, was a poor leader. A former First World War pilot, he had been severely wounded in the Munich Putsch and had become addicted to his medicinal drugs, which led to some erratic decisions. Germany also lacked a sophisticated radar system.

What was the strength of the RAF?

In July 1940 its front-line strength was 1,200 planes. It had 660 operational Hurricane and Spitfire single-seater fighters, which was about equal to the Luftwaffe fighter units.

Britain had good reserves of planes but not of experienced pilots. The morale of the RAF was high. It had a good chain of command, headed by a respected and able Commander-in-Chief, Air Marshal Dowding, and his second-in-command, Air Marshal Park.

Britain's Radio Direction Finding (RDF) system, which was based on radar, was revolutionary. Reflecting radio rays detected the position of distant objects and enabled the outnumbered British aircraft to turn up at the right place at the right time to intercept the majority of Luftwaffe raids. The defence system was backed up by the Royal Army Ordnance Corps (RAOC), whose members tracked planes with binoculars from various look-outs and used anti-aircraft guns, barrage balloons (which prevented low-level attacks) and powerful searchlights.

▲ A Spitfire (in the foreground) and a Hurricane

UK	2,429	Canadian	90	Belgian	29	South African	21	American	
Polish	141	Czechoslovakian	86	Australian	21	French	13	Others	
New Zealand	102								

Nationalities of RAF pilots

The Battle of Britain

"NEVER WAS SO MUCH OWED BY SO MANY TO SO FEW"
THE PRIME MINISTER

▲ A Battle of Britain poster

1940	
10 July	Luftwaffe test tactics and capacities of fighters by attacking shipping in Straits of Dover.
13 August	Germans launch Operation Eagle, an air offensive to destroy resistance of Fighter Command. RAF airfields, radar stations and aircraft factories attacked.
15 August	Main battle begins. German daily losses higher except for one day.
23 August to 6 September	Critical stage for Britain. Heavy damage on ground. Six out of seven main (sector) airfields damaged. Operations Room and all communications wrecked at Biggin Hill (sector headquarters). Flow of new pilots and planes fell short of losses. New pilots inevitably inexperienced. Exhausted, outnumbered pilots often had to cede height and position to enemy. Britain close to losing battle. Hitler, however, orders change of tactics.

Why did he do that?

A lost German plane mistakenly dropped a bomb on London. Churchill ordered retaliatory raids on Berlin. Hitler, enraged, ordered raids on London.

7 September	Beginning of the Blitz on London. 372 bombers and 672 fighters attack on this day, killing 1,000 people. This diversion, though, enabled RAF to recover strength.
11 September	German invasion craft move to action stations. 'Invasion imminent' warning issued.
15 September	Final major engagement of Battle of Britain. Germany fails to win clear victory and loses 60 aircraft to Britain's 25. Total losses: Luftwaffe 1,733, RAF 915.
17 September	Hitler postpones Operation Sea Lion 'until further notice'.
October	German invasion transport removed from French Channel ports.

The Battle of Britain was a decisive battle in the history of the British people. Churchill commented: 'Never in the field of human conflict was so much owed by so many to so few.'

Battle of Britain and Blitz	First phase: convoys attacked	Second phase: Operation Eagle air offensive	Main battle begins	Third phase: beginning of Blitz	Battle of Britain day	Fourth phase: end of Battle of Britain	Operation Sea Lion cancelled	End of Blitz
	1940 July 10	August 13	August 15	September 7	September 15	September 30	October	1941 May

The Blitz

When and where did air raids take place?

Mostly at night and chiefly over London.

Londoners were bombed on 76 out of 77 days and endured bombing from a nightly average of 200 planes. The East End suffered particularly badly. The Chamber of the House of Commons was destroyed and Buckingham Palace was hit while George VI and Queen Elizabeth were in residence. Ports such as Swansea, Plymouth and Liverpool were obvious targets, as were industrial cities such as Manchester, Sheffield and Glasgow. In the Midlands, the manufacturing city of Coventry, which was producing war materials, was subjected to a massive raid from 450 planes. On November 15, 1940, in a ten-hour period, more than a third of the city was destroyed and over 1,000 people killed. The destruction of the city's cathedral, built between 1373 and 1450, was keenly felt. Nevertheless, within five days, all the factories were in full production again. Air raid wardens throughout the country made sure that the blackout, in which even lighting a match in the street was an offence, was total. Blitz wardens directed people to safety. Thousands of Londoners slept in Underground stations, but most people stayed in their own homes or used Anderson shelters, which were made of steel plates and could be erected in gardens.

By the end of the Blitz in May 1941, 30,000 people had been killed, 2 million made homeless and 3.5 million houses had been damaged or destroyed. Despite the risk, discomfort, strain and injuries suffered, the morale of the British people remained high. Churchill asserted: 'This was their finest hour.'

▲ Wardens checking an Anderson shelter

Food rationing: typical weekly amounts per person (1oz = approx 25g)	Bacon: 6oz Cheese: 4oz	Butter: 4oz Sweets: 3oz	Sugar: 12oz Tea: 3oz	Milk: 1 pint Eggs: 2	Dried milk: 4 pints Dried eggs: 12 every 8 weeks	16 points every 4 weeks for luxury items, e.g. tinned fruit

1940 January 8

Women at war

▲ An all-women crew hoist a barrage balloon

Air raid wardens were part of the Civil Defence Organisation run by local authorities. Included in this were the Auxiliary Fire Service, Auxiliary Police Corps, the Red Cross, St John's Ambulance Brigade and Women's Voluntary Service (WVS). Many women volunteered to join the Civil Defence or the Land Army, re-formed in 1939. Others worked for the auxiliary forces such as the WRNS and WAAF. Though not allowed in combat, women worked alongside men, directing searchlights, filling sandbags or acting as radio controllers. Women pilots were allowed to ferry aircraft from factories to RAF airfields. Others worked in the intelligence services and a few as secret agents, which was lonely and dangerous work behind enemy lines.

Most jobs undertaken by women during the war were repetitive and boring, but women who took over work traditionally regarded as men's – welding, forging and precision engineering – became equally skilled, though less well paid. In 1941 conscription was introduced for unmarried women aged between 20 and 50. By 1943, 90 per cent of unmarried and 8 per cent of married women were doing work of national importance.

Meanwhile, a woman's role in Germany was different. There, the slogan Kinder, Kirche, Küche (Children, Church, Kitchen), which had been adopted by the Nazis, promoted the place of women in the home.

In addition, all British families were rationed. Food was rationed from January 1940 and clothes from June 1941. By 1942, 48 clothing coupons had to last an adult man a year.

What could they buy?

Two coupons bought one pair of stockings. Eighteen coupons were needed to buy one lined woollen coat. People learned to 'make do and mend'.

peal for Local fence Volunteers DV) aged 17 to 65	1,456,000 registered volunteers	Men over 70 complain that they are not allowed to fight for their country	Churchill changes LDV name to Home Guard	Tasks included traffic control, garrison duties and clearing raid debris
40 May 14	June		July	

The Home Guard

A women's auxiliary unit was formed to help the Home Guard in its defence of the realm against possible enemy seaborne or airborne invasions. The response to the May 1940 call for volunteers had been so enthusiastic that equipment and military uniforms were in short supply. This did not deter the recruits, some of whom turned up for training with packets of pepper, chair legs, garden tools, cutlasses, and ancient muskets and cannon (without ammunition) ransacked from museums. Some units received rifles from First World War stocks sent by the USA and Canada. When uniforms – khaki denim two-piece overalls – did arrive, the lack of variety in sizes caused irritation to the wearers and much merriment amongst observers.

Some over-zealous volunteers, nervously expecting the enemy to drop from the sky at any moment, did sometimes mistake clouds, stray barrage balloons and white puffs of anti-aircraft shell-burst for parachutes. Strange, flickering lights, thought to be signals from spies to enemy aircraft, turned out to be, on one occasion, two glow-worms. Furtive movements in the undergrowth, which did not respond to the command 'Halt! Who goes there?', were often revealed to be cows, sheep – even hedgehogs! Church bells, the chosen invasion alarm, were rung rather frequently at first.

▲ Members of the Dover Home Guard demonstrate camouflage techniques

How effective was the Home Guard?

Despite being the target of good-natured humour, it did, in fact, support the war effort in valuable ways.

It allowed thousands of specialist troops such as signallers and gunners to be transferred elsewhere. By 1944, over 118,000 members had been trained to man anti-aircraft guns and rocket batteries. Others were involved in coastal defence, minefield maintenance and auxiliary bomb-disposal work. Perhaps its greatest effect was in boosting wartime morale.

Mussolini declares war on Britain and France	Italy invades Egypt	Italy invades Greece	Britain takes Cyrenaica	Germany takes Cyrenaica	Germany overthrows Yugoslavia	Germany takes Greece	Germany takes Crete	Germany keeps Cyrenaica
1940 June 10	September 13	October 28	1941 February	April		May	June	June 15

Mussolini enters the war

At the height of the Blitz, British soldiers were chiefly engaged in fighting in the North African desert.

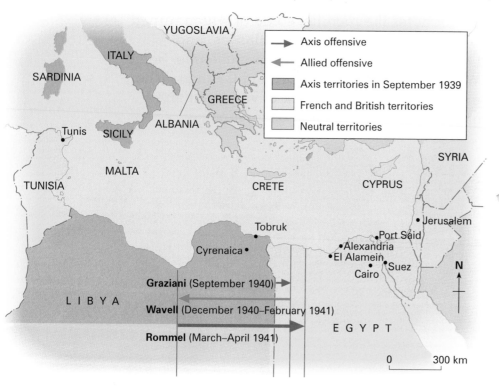

▲ War in North Africa and the Mediterranean, 1940–1941

Why there?

Mussolini had declared war against Britain and France in June 1940, when he realised that France would fall and anticipated that Britain would follow. Craving military successes to match those of Hitler, Mussolini dreamt of recreating the glories of the Roman Empire.

On September 13 troops from the Italian colony of Libya in Africa invaded the British protectorate of Egypt. Although outnumbered ten to one, the British drove the Italians halfway back into Libya. In January 1941 Tobruk was occupied and, by February 8, the whole of Cyrenaica was in British hands. Hitler intervened to help his ally. General Rommel and a tank division (later the Afrika Corps) were sent to Tripoli in Libya. The British, expecting an offensive in June, attacked Rommel on March 30. By April 11 Britain had lost all gains in Cyrenaica and kept only a garrison in Tobruk.

In October 1940 Mussolini had also ordered Italian troops based in Albania to invade Greece. Hitler, concerned that Britain (which had guaranteed to help Greece) might establish air bases there and threaten his oilfields in Romania, again intervened. To reach Greece, the Germans overthrew Yugoslavia, something which only took a week. By the end of April resistance on the Greek mainland was over and the Greek island of Crete – inadequately defended by the Allies against an airborne invasion – fell in June.

On June 15 the British tried to drive Rommel out of Cyrenaica and relieve Tobruk. After three days and with a loss of 91 tanks to Germany's 12, the battle was broken off. On June 22 Hitler now turned from these 'sideshows', as he viewed them, to direct the invasion of Russia.

	3,200,000 German soldiers advance along 1,500km front	2,000,000 Russian soldiers and 2,200,000 reserves to defend	Luftwaffe had 3,000 planes, Soviet air force had 6,000 (although many were outdated)	Russians had few spare parts, no ground control; shortage of radios
ermany vades ussia				

41 June 22

Operation Barbarossa

Why did Hitler invade Russia?

Because he was confident of victory!

Hitler dismissed the Soviet army as technically outdated and its commanders – since Stalin's purges – as men without leadership qualities.

There were other reasons behind his decision. He saw Russia as a threat and did not want her to intervene to help Britain. The Nazi–Soviet pact had been a convenient alliance. He had no intention now of allowing Russia to keep eastern Poland. He detested communism. He wanted more 'living space' for the superior Aryan race. He regarded the Russian Slavs as inferior people who bred like vermin. He needed the resources that Russia had in plenty: oil from the Caucasus, wheat from the Ukraine and the slave labour to work for Germany.

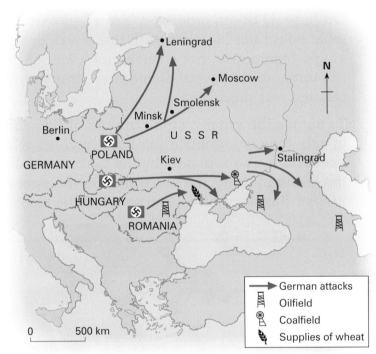

▲ The German invasion plan

He thought, furthermore, that once Russia was defeated, Britain would negotiate for peace. The invasion plan, Operation Barbarossa, was based on Blitzkrieg tactics and a three-pronged attack was chosen. In the north, Leningrad was the target; in the centre, Moscow; and in the south, the Ukraine and then the Caucasus.

So confident was Hitler of victory that only a month's major combat supplies were issued to troops. Stalin, despite intelligence reports, information from deserters and warnings from Britain and the USA that invasion was imminent, failed to heed the danger. The force that launched the surprise attack on June 22, 1941 was the most powerful ever assembled in Europe up to that time.

On the first day, a quarter of the Russian air force (about 1,500 of 6,000 aircraft, mostly on the ground) was destroyed. By the 18th day the German Panzers had advanced 560km. Whole armies surrendered and cities fell. But the Russian people refused to give up their motherland to the Germans.

War in Russia

What did Stalin do?

He appealed immediately to Britain for aid. Both Britain and the USA, wanting above all else the defeat of Germany, put aside their distrust of communism and sent supplies.

On June 29 Stalin ordered a 'scorched earth' policy. As troops and civilians retreated, what could not be taken with them was destroyed, 'leaving the enemy with not a single locomotive, not a truck, not a loaf of bread, not a litre of fuel'. Factories were not torched: they were dismantled, transported east to safety and re-erected to resume war production.

To harass the enemy, small groups of Russian partisans were left behind with orders to sabotage communication links such as telegraph and telephone wires. If caught, executions and reprisals by the Germans followed. It was the excessive brutality of the German army, the shootings on the spot of peasants and prisoners of war, that fuelled Russian hatred and swelled the ranks of partisans.

▲ A Russian partisan lights a fuse to destroy a Nazi train

With too many prisoners – an estimated three million by September – to cope with, the Germans herded many into crude compounds of barbed wire with no cover and deliberately left the men to starve. Working alongside the army were the SS special units, rooting out and hunting down Jewish families, with orders to kill. This was the real beginning of the Holocaust, the mass murder of Jews. Tens of thousands were slaughtered in Russia alone.

Meanwhile, on July 16 the last line of defence before Moscow was broken and serious bombing of the capital could begin. Hitler anticipated a great victory. Russia was within his grasp. Yet the Russians still fought back tenaciously.

ege of Leningrad 00 days)	Kiev (capital of Ukraine) taken	Jews from Kiev: 33,771 killed in 3 days near Babi Yar	Operation Typhoon begins (capture of Moscow)	German troops 1,100–1,600km from bases	German front line halted before Moscow
41 September	September 19		October 2		December 5

Into the space and snow

At the end of July 1941 the German advance paused to re-fit. As it moved from west to east, it had spread out like a fan from north to south into the vast Russian expanses. Supplies were taking longer to reach the armies. The Luftwaffe was too small in numbers to cover a new front of 3,200km.

Army commanders wanted to press on and take the capital, Moscow, before the onset of winter. Hitler ordered the two outer 'prongs' to overcome their opposing armies first before uniting to advance on the city.

In the north, Leningrad was ready to be taken. Hitler decided on a siege to starve the people into surrender. In the south, the Ukraine was conquered. Yet it was early October before the attack on Moscow resumed. By then the first flurries of snow had fallen. In mid-October sleet and rain halted the advance by creating heavy mudded tracks, often impassable for tanks.

▲ Winter snow, -38°C

As the mud froze over, the German tanks could move once more. Men, however, began to develop frostbite. By December temperatures had dropped so sharply that machines, with no anti-freeze, came to a standstill. Guns could not fire. Severe frostbite made amputations necessary. With inadequate and insufficient clothing, soldiers began to freeze to death. Some committed suicide. Then, on December 5 a Russian counter-attack was launched. Using ski-troop battalions, sturdy Cossack ponies, men equipped for winter warfare in white camouflage suits and machines that worked in blizzard conditions, the Russians forced a German retreat. Moscow was saved. This was a turning point in the war.

Why?

Blitzkrieg had failed. Hitler, to keep the initiative, now had to think in terms of a long war, no longer a short one.

123

2 million Jews in Polish ghettos	Nacht und Nebel (Night and Fog) decree	Nazis plan systematic destruction of all European Jews	Extermination camps took Jews, prisoners of war, gypsies, Resistance workers, German opponents of Hitler, the mentally and physically handicapped
1941	December	1942 January 20	

Into the night and fog

That same winter of 1941, as the Germans and their starving prisoners froze to death in Russia, freezing temperatures and starvation were killing thousands of Jews in the Polish ghettos. Earlier in the year, the Nazi High Command had decided on a 'general solution' to dispose of the Jews.

▲ The one-way railway line to Auschwitz

The preferred method emerging was not mass shootings on the spot but deportation to remote locations and death by gas in special vans or chambers. Successful tests had been carried out that autumn in Auschwitz using a commercial pesticide, Zyklan B. At the first of these extermination camps, Chelmo, Jews from surrounding villages and the Lodz ghetto, together with 7,000 gypsies, were gassed in vans at the rate of a thousand a day until 300,000 had been murdered.

Jews from the Warsaw ghetto, now dying at a rate of 4,000 a month, had to wait for their journey to a death camp until Treblinka had been completed. To disguise the true nature of this operation, written instructions were carefully worded. The Jews ('merchandise') were herded into cattle trucks ('resettlement trains'). The journey to the death camps was called 'transportation of Jews towards the Russian East'. The waiting gas vans were the product of 'technical modification of special vehicles'.

Jews were not the only ones who were to perish in large numbers in extermination camps. On December 7, 1941 Hitler issued a top secret Nacht und Nebel (Night and Fog) decree. Any persons 'endangering German security' for political, national or racial reasons were to 'vanish without trace into the night and fog' – the oblivion of any one of these terrible camps.

Pearl Harbor

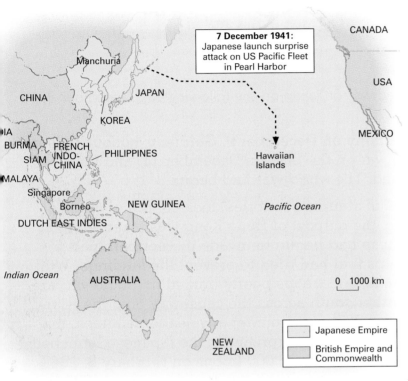

South-East Asia in 1941, showing the location of Pearl Harbor

Map labels: CANADA, USA, MEXICO, Hawaiian Islands, Pacific Ocean, JAPAN, KOREA, CHINA, Manchuria, BURMA, SIAM, FRENCH INDO-CHINA, PHILIPPINES, MALAYA, Singapore, Borneo, DUTCH EAST INDIES, NEW GUINEA, Indian Ocean, AUSTRALIA, NEW ZEALAND

7 December 1941: Japanese launch surprise attack on US Pacific Fleet in Pearl Harbor

0 1000 km

Japanese Empire
British Empire and Commonwealth

An act of aggression by Japan against the USA turned this European war into world war.

How did that occur?

Japan, having already occupied much of China, wanted to expand her empire by conquering the whole of Asia.

She aimed to make herself self-sufficient in vital raw materials such as oil and rubber. Valuable commodities like these could be found in British, Dutch and French colonies south of Japan. Once war in Europe began, these countries were too busy to defend effectively their colonial territories.

In December 1940 the USA, aware of Japanese interest in these colonies and wanting to protect her own trading concerns in Asia, began to block sales of war materials to Japan. In July 1941 Japan, taking advantage of the fall of France, took control of French Indo-China (Vietnam).

Roosevelt, the American President, responded firmly and seized Japanese assets in the USA. Britain and Holland followed, seizing Japanese assets in *their* territories. Japan was now deprived of 90 per cent of her oil imports.

As talks took place with the USA to solve the dispute, six Japanese aircraft carriers sailed undetected across the Pacific towards Pearl Harbor in Hawaii, a key American naval base. The plan was to destroy the US Pacific Fleet there and conquer South-East Asia before the Americans could rebuild their navy. In a two-hour attack early on Sunday, December 7, 1941, 353 Japanese planes sank 8 battleships, destroyed 350 aircraft and killed 3,581 forces personnel. Three aircraft carriers, which were absent on manoeuvres, escaped destruction. As a surprise offensive, this had been impressive, though as war had not been declared, it was a criminal act.

Japanese gains in South-East Asia	Guam Island: US naval base	Wake Island: US naval base	Hong Kong: British colony	Malaya and Singapore: British colonies	Dutch East Indies	Burma: British colony	Philippines: US-controlled	Part ◁ New Guine
1941–1942	December 10	December 22	December 25	1942 February	March to April	April	May	July

World war

> What happened as a result of this attack?

> Both the USA and Britain declared war on Japan on the following day, December 8.

China declared war on Japan and Germany on December 9. Germany, honouring her military alliance with Japan, declared war on the USA on December 11, and Italy – a member of the same alliance – followed. The *world* war had begun.

Within three months Japan, in a series of stunning victories, took control of much of South-East Asia. Of the British Empire, the outpost of Hong Kong was taken first, on December 25, 1941. By then the Japanese had begun to invade the northern part of Malaya, sinking the two British warships that had tried to prevent the landings. With insufficient and inferior aircraft, no tanks, and troops poorly trained in jungle warfare, the Allies were pushed further and further south across the causeway onto the island of Singapore, the vital British naval base. There, to counter any seaborne attack, the fixed gun batteries could fire only out to sea. Not surprisingly, the Japanese launched their attack by land, from the rear as it were, with 35,000 troops on February 8, 1942.

One week later, with water supplies cut off, artillery ammunition almost exhausted and no reserves of petrol left, the island surrendered. All 80,000 defenders – British, Australian and Indian soldiers – became prisoners of war.

The loss of Singapore was a huge blow to the prestige of Britain as a world power. A successful Japanese invasion of Burma followed. Sixty thousand British soldiers retreated 1,600km to Assam on the Indian frontier to fight another day.

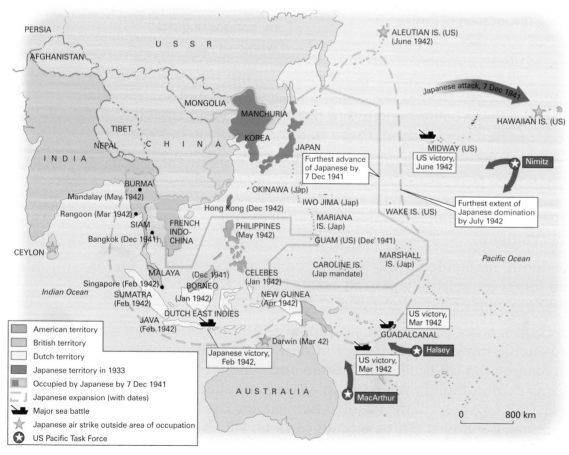

▲ War in the Pacific, 1941–1942

...tle of ...ral Sea	USA gain knowledge of Japanese cipher messages	USA and Japan both lose a carrier each	Battle of Midway	Japan puts to sea: 21 submarines, 11 battleships, 8 carriers, 22 cruisers, 65 destroyers	USA sends: 3 carriers, 8 cruisers, 17 destroyers
...2 May 8			June 4		

Japanese successes halted

MAJOR
25
TURNING POINTS

With additional conquests of the Dutch East Indies in March 1942, followed by the taking of the American-controlled Philippines in May, Japan completed her roll-call of victories in South-East Asia.

She now controlled all the world's rubber, 70 per cent of its tin and the oil from the Dutch East Indies. The fear now was that Japan might look for *further* conquests. The British feared for India and Ceylon (now Sri Lanka), the Australians for Port Darwin.

The Japanese, in fact, decided to occupy Port Moresby in Papua New Guinea, which was within striking distance of Australia. At this point, however, the USA began to exact revenge for the assault on Pearl Harbor. At the Battle of Coral Sea on May 8, 1942 the two forces 'met' without ships seeing enemy ships or exchanging gunfire!

How?

For the first time, a naval battle was conducted entirely by aircraft taking off from aircraft carriers positioned 160km apart.

Each side had two carriers: each lost one. The Japanese, alarmed at America's rapid recovery after Pearl Harbor, broke off the encounter. At the ensuing Battle of Midway in June 1942 the Japanese, determined to crush the American navy, launched a huge armada that included 8 carriers and 11 battleships. Yet, in the space of five minutes, US planes sank four of those carriers and destroyed 330 aircraft. The feared battleships never saw action. From now on, the essential component in naval warfare was the aircraft carrier. Both sides had the same number then. Nine months later the USA had 19 carriers against Japan's ten. Japan was now thrown into the defensive.

▲ USS *Saratoga* (CV3) aircraft carrier, which joined the US fleet after the Battle of Midway

Battle of Stalingrad	German 6th Army trapped	Airlift begins, few tonnes dropped	Russians offer Paulus honourable terms for surrender	Hitler insists on no surrender	Paulus surrenders	91,000 prisoners taken, 6,000 returned
1942 September 13	November	November 25	1943 January 8		February 1	

Stalingrad

In June 1942 on the Eastern Front, Hitler still held the initiative. Russian counter-attacks in May had ended in complete failure.

Did the Germans take Moscow?

No. Hitler concentrated his summer offensive on the Caucasus to take the oilfields and on Stalingrad, the city of Stalin, desiring the prestige the capture of this city would give him.

▲ The last stand for the Germans before the liberation of Stalingrad

Stalingrad, straggling 30km along the River Volga, could not be encircled or besieged. It had to be taken by direct assault. On September 13, 1942 the German 6th Army under General Paulus launched an all-out air and ground attack. Four weeks later the Russian 62nd Army under General Chuikov was desperately defending a bridgehead only $4\frac{1}{2}$km deep around three large factories – all that was left to hold. After 15 days of uninterrupted savage combat, often hand-to-hand, the Russians were holding a bridgehead reduced to just over a kilometre. By mid November, floating ice on the River Volga prevented reinforcements reaching General Chuikov but he stood firm. Then, at last, the Russians managed a counter-offensive, which swept round the German 6th Army, defeating flanking divisions and cutting off 220,000 men. Hitler rejected the idea of an immediate attempt at break-out by the surrounded and trapped 6th Army, relying on supply by air and an eventual relief force. The Luftwaffe, however, flying now in winter conditions, dropped insufficient tonnage and the relief force could not reach far enough.

When General Paulus eventually surrendered on February 1, 70,000 Germans had died – many from disease, exposure, starvation and suicide – in this most dreadful of sieges. But, for the Russians, Stalingrad was an important victory. They now felt they could win their great patriotic war.

ttle of Alamein	Allied forces: 195,000 men, more than 1,000 tanks	German–Italian forces: 104,000 men, 500 tanks	Allied losses: 13,000 men, 430 tanks	German–Italian losses: 59,000 men including prisoners, 500 tanks, 400 guns

42 October 23 to November 3

El Alamein

The Allies continued to send supplies to support Russia and, by extending war in North Africa, forced Hitler to divert men and resources there. General Rommel (the Desert Fox), despite being pushed back into Libya late in 1941, soon seized the initiative again. In January 1942 he pushed the British 8th Army (the Desert Rats) back to the lines at Gazala and in one day, June 20, took Tobruk. With 35,000 captured prisoners and invaluable supplies, he remained on the offensive. The 8th Army, however, then managed to defeat Rommel at what became known as the first Battle of El Alamein, but when a second attack to destroy the Axis forces failed, a new commander, General Montgomery, was appointed.

Montgomery halted Rommel's bid to reach the River Nile at the Battle of Alam el Halfa in August, and, with Rommel invalided home, began meticulous preparations for another encounter.

He made excellent use of British intelligence. He demanded and got extra men and supplies, including 300 Sherman tanks and Flying Fortresses (B17 bombers) from the USA. On October 23, 1942, under cover of an elaborate deception plan, he took the enemy by surprise, using his full strength against them. Rommel, rushing back from Germany at Hitler's request, found that the battle was already lost. When his counter-attack failed, he was forced to withdraw. This second Battle of El Alamein was a resounding victory for the Allies.

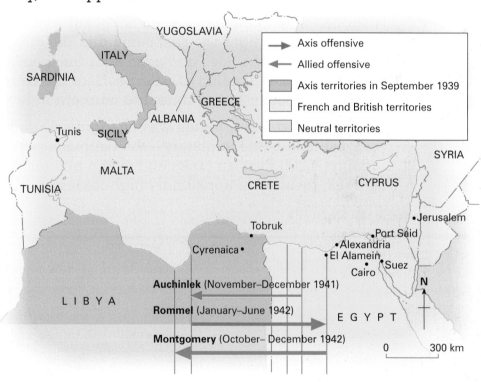

▲ War in North Africa and the Mediterranean, 1941–1942

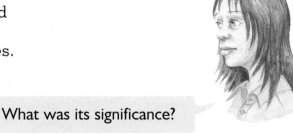

What was its significance?

It was Britain's first real victory over Germany on land. It paved the way for the next step in the struggle for the Mediterranean and a toehold in Europe.

Operation Torch: Allied invasion of North Africa	Axis forces surrender in North Africa	Battle of Kursk: Russian victory	Allied invasion of Sicily	Mussolini dismissed	Italians surrender	Allied landings in Italy	Italians join Allies	Russian advance Smolensk and Kiev retaken
1942 November 9	**1943** May 13	July 5–12	July 10	July 25	September 3		October 13	August to December

From defensive to offensive

As General Rommel retreated to Tunisia, a planned Anglo–American invasion in North Africa, Operation Torch, took place on November 9, 1942. By the time the Allies had begun to advance, Rommel had been joined by fresh German and Italian forces brought in by sea and air. Rommel struck back, defeating the Americans in February 1943 but being defeated by the 8th Army under Montgomery in March. Then, on May 13, with no longer enough fuel to ensure supplies, the Axis forces surrendered.

The Mediterranean was now open to Allied shipping. The next step towards gaining a toehold in Europe was an invasion of Sicily. With Italy thus threatened, the Italian king dismissed Mussolini on July 25, marking the end of fascism in that country. After negotiation with the Italians, an act of surrender was signed on September 3, leaving the Germans to fight on. That same day, the 8th Army invaded the Italian mainland, landing first in the 'toe', and soon after the 'heel', of Italy. This was followed by a larger American landing at Salerno. Here the Germans counter-attacked but, when this failed, began a slow retreat to northern Italy.

In Russia, too, the situation was changing. On July 5, 1943 at the Battle of Kursk – the biggest tank battle in history – the Germans pitted 2,500 tanks and 700,000 men against 4,000 Russian tanks and over a million men. This ferocious encounter, lasting a week, resulted in appallingly high losses on both sides, but it was the Russians who held the field and began to advance. The Battle of Kursk, with those of Moscow and Stalingrad, was the third and last decisive battle on the Eastern Front and marked the beginning of a slow German retreat homewards. The Allies were now very much on the offensive.

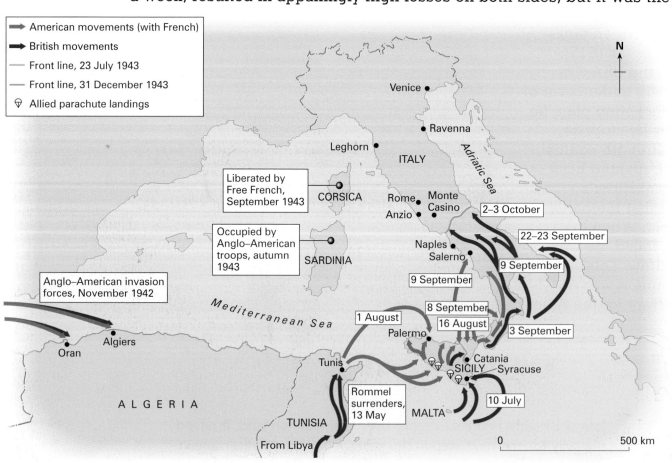

▲ The invasion of Italy, 1943

schwitz banded Final lution	First gassings	When all 4 chambers working, 4,000 Jews a day could be gassed	Death transports brought: 400,000 Jews from Hungary 250,000 Jews from Poland and Upper Silesia 100,000 Jews from Germany	90,000 Jews from the Netherlands 90,000 Jews from Slovakia 65,000 Jews from Greece 11,000 Jews from France
42 March	June 23			

The Final Solution

Despite German military setbacks, the Jewish elimination programme was progressing. The general solution – the mass death of Jews by gassing rather than shooting – was adopted, and, by early 1942, had become the Final Solution. Auschwitz was chosen to be a dual-purpose establishment. By building an extension at nearby Birkenau, it became both a slave labour and a death camp. From March 31, 1942 as Jewish families arrived they were divided into two groups: fit to work or 'unfit'.

During the next 2½ years, more than half of over a million Jews who had been transported to Auschwitz were murdered in one of four specially constructed gas chambers with crematoria attached. Procedures in all the death camps were similar:

• Suitcases and bundles were taken away on arrival.

• Clothing was taken from prisoners.

• Women's heads were shaved (the hair was used to make mattresses).

• People queued for a 'shower' in the chamber.

• Once inside and the doors having been locked, the jets in the ceiling released poison gas from a prussic acid crystal – Zyklan B.

• Death took between 3 and 15 minutes.

• Gold teeth were extracted and rings removed before cremation.

The Nazis made enormous profits from the sale of this gold and other items such as watches, fur coats and spectacles confiscated before death. Helping to choose who should live or die at Auschwitz was an SS doctor, Joseph Mengele. He also selected suitable patients for his experiments without anaesthetic. He practised on young women and others to find the best medical means of multiplying the pure Aryan race. Most died. Some did live to tell their story.

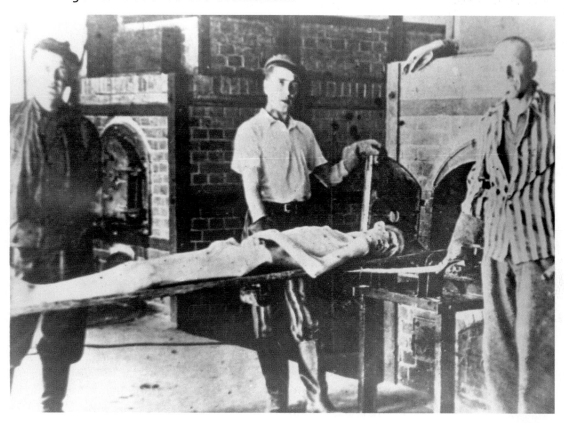

▲ The crematoria at Dachau

Resistance movements in every occupied country	France: Free French under Charles de Gaulle	Russia: partisans grew to over half a million	Yugoslavia: partisans under Marshal Tito

1939–1945

26 Resistance

Resistance to the Nazi regime took many forms, from individual acts of disobedience to organised conspiracies and assassination attempts on Nazi leaders. For individuals in Germany, it was difficult to express any form of dissent as the Gestapo had many willing paid and unpaid informers. Refusing to utter the greeting 'Heil Hitler' or making remarks that the war might be lost risked grave consequences, even death. Those in the strongest position in Germany to overthrow the regime were the army generals, many of whom became alarmed at Hitler's reckless military judgements and brutality towards the Jews. On July 20, 1944 an army general, Colonel von Stauffenberg, after several unsuccessful assassination attempts, nearly succeeded. A briefcase containing a bomb, which he left under a table in the conference room at Nazi headquarters in East Prussia, did explode. Hitler, protected by the heavy table, was only slightly hurt. Stauffenberg and his fellow conspirators were executed.

Resistance was present in various forms in every occupied country too. In Denmark, for example, the king, Christian X, began to wear the same armband that Danish Jews had been ordered to wear. Soon, practically every man, woman and child wore one too. The order was dropped. Organised Resistance movements in occupied countries carried out sabotage and other activities such as the secret printing of anti-Nazi leaflets. German soldiers found dealing with guerrilla warfare waged by resisters such as Greek shepherds and Norwegian reindeer herdsmen – who knew their own terrain intimately – difficult.

What happened if resisters were caught?

Death and reprisals generally followed capture.

▲ Three Russian partisans before their execution in Minsk. The placard reads 'We are the partisans who shot at German troops'.

Pencil-sized time fuses delayed detonation	Microprints in collar studs	One-man submarine carrying explosive charge	Foldaway motorbike to put in parachute container	Explosive woodcarvings and books	Wireless transmitters disguised as vacuum cleaners

OE devices

The SOE

The Special Operations Executive, created by the War Cabinet in July 1940, was an off-shoot of the secret service MI6 and was set up to help the Resistance in German-occupied countries. It expanded to about 10,000 men and women who were engaged 'in the field' to carry out sabotage missions behind enemy lines. Although some senior ministers at Whitehall did not take the SOE seriously, Churchill had no doubts about its potential and urged agents to 'set Europe ablaze'.

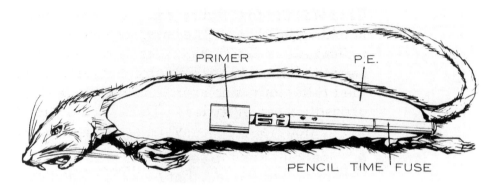

▲ Explosive rats

What did agents do?

They had to be prepared to undertake what, in peace time, would be considered criminal activity – deceptions, bribery, forgery of passports, acts of sabotage, even assassination.

Trainee recruits were taught activities such as how to force locks, use fuses and detonators and practise unarmed and armed combat. They had the use of various ingenious devices. Rat skins were cured, filled and armed with explosive devices. These were hidden in piles of coal near boilers. When thrown into the boiler by unsuspecting janitors, the heat of the flames would set off the fuse. All agents knew that, if captured, torture and death would very likely follow, so they carried suicide pills. Some agents were betrayed by fellow countrymen or double-agents.

While some operations were amateurish or unrealistic, others were well planned. The progress of German atomic research, for example, was delayed by Norwegian SOE agents who, in a daring raid at Germany's only manufacturing plant in Norway, put out of action containers of 'heavy water' – a substance used in nuclear research. These agents, like so many others, were prepared to risk their lives in the defeat of Nazism.

▲ Time bombs disguised as wine bottles

Codebreakers move to Bletchley Park, Buckinghamshire	Enigma machine: six million million million possible permutations for every letter	Colossus Mark I: world's first electronically controlled digital computer	First open reference to Ultra permitted
1941 June		1943	1974

Ultra, Enigma and Colossus

Ultra was the first British wartime cover-name used from June 1941 for all high-grade signals intelligence. The work was carried out at Government Communications Headquarters (GCHQ) at Bletchley Park and outstations at home and abroad. Ultra's main task was to break, interpret and summarise signals of the Axis powers (Germany, Italy and Japan) and distribute them to Allied commanders in Britain and abroad.

About 100 codebreakers began work in 1939, but by 1944 more than 7,000 were employed in this top secret work without the Germans ever knowing of their existence and the fact that Axis messages were being deciphered.

As early as the end of 1942, Ultra, working round the clock, was reading some 4,000 high-grade German signals a day, with slightly smaller numbers of Italian and Japanese signals. Enigma was the actual machine used in various forms by the German armed services and government departments solely to encipher and decipher messages. To break the top priority signals sent out on another machine, the Geheheimschreiber (secret writer), codebreakers used Colossus, the world's first electronically controlled digital computer, which was developed with British expertise.

▲ Part of Colossus (probably Mark II) being adjusted by Wrens

Did Ultra influence the course of the war?

Undoubtedly. Allied commanders came to rely on the summaries they received. As they learned of enemy intentions, such as disposal of troops, they could plan their own strategies.

The value of intelligence lies in how well it is used to defeat the enemy. Ultra had direct effects on land campaigns and on the war at sea – in the Pacific, the Mediterranean and the Atlantic.

	1939	1940	1941	1942	1943	1944	1945
U-boat losses	9	22	35	85	287	241	153
Allied ship losses	810	4,407	4,398	8,245	3,611	1,422	458

The Battle of the Atlantic

As in the First World War, the main threat to Britain's physical and economic survival was unrestricted warfare by German U-boats in the Atlantic. It was essential that the 3,000 ocean-going merchant ships – which imported every gallon of oil, half of Britain's food and most of industry's raw materials, as well as exporting manufactured goods – should be protected.

How did Ultra help?

At first, not at all. Codebreakers were unable to break the German Enigma naval code. Meanwhile, British signals were being read by the enemy, causing devastation to Allied shipping.

In one month alone, February 1940, losses approached a quarter of a million tonnes, two-thirds of which were sunk by ten operational U-boats. The Allies, admittedly, had sunk about 12 U-boats since September 1939. Allied convoys at this time had insufficient escort vessels and aircraft to protect them. Since they covered large areas – 45 ships in nine columns would spread over 50 square kilometres – they were vulnerable to attack.

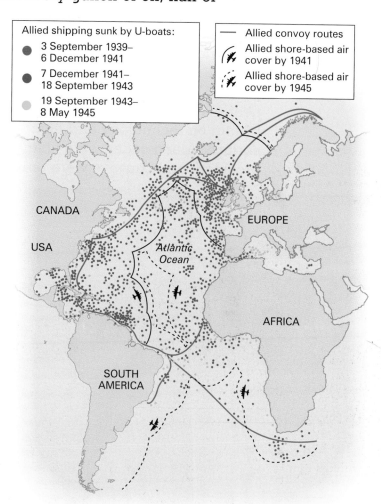

Allied shipping sunk by U-boats:
- 3 September 1939–6 December 1941
- 7 December 1941–18 September 1943
- 19 September 1943–8 May 1945

— Allied convoy routes
Allied shore-based air cover by 1941
Allied shore-based air cover by 1945

▲ The Battle of the Atlantic, 1939–1945

Britain did develop sonic (ASDIC) techniques that could detect German U-boats under water, but from September 1940 Doenitz, the outstanding commander of U-boats, introduced a new tactic – the hunting of convoys by 'wolf packs'. Groups of up to 40 U-boats shadowed by day and attacked at night on the surface when free from sonic detection.

The Germans called the time from July 1940 to March 1941, when over a million tonnes of shipping were sunk, 'happy times'. But these were worrying times for Churchill. At least he was helped by a supply of 50 reconditioned First World War destroyers from the USA, a re-thinking of anti-submarine tactics. Then came a breakthrough in Ultra.

863 U-boats sailed, 754 were sunk	39,000 men sailed in U-boats: 27,000 died, 5,000 taken as prisoners of war	Allies lost 30,248 merchant seamen and thousands of Royal Navy and RAF men	2,603 merchant ships lost, plus 175 naval vessels

1939–1945 The Battle of the Atlantic

'Happy times' again

A naval Enigma machine with ciphers and current rotor settings was captured in May 1941. Consequently, intelligence from Bletchley did help Allied commanders plan attack and defence tactics. But there were setbacks. The entry of the USA into the war in December 1941 coincided with a change in Enigma codes and a ten-month blackout of Allied intelligence summaries. With no convoy system, American shipping losses were at first high. The Germans called the time from January to August 1942, when they again sank over a million tonnes of Allied shipping, their second 'happy time'. They were also building up their original fleet of 57 U-boats to nearly 400. Once the USA adopted the convoy system, however, she worked with Britain on technology and tactics. Radar was developed to detect submarines on the surface, Allied codes were changed, more air cover and escort vessels were provided, and convoys were re-routed around 'wolf pack' patrol lines.

▲ Part of a North Sea convoy carrying supplies to Soviet Russia

To force U-boats to submerge and so use up battery power, depth charges were dropped. As submarines surfaced to recharge their batteries, the escorts were waiting to destroy them.

By May 1943 Doenitz realised he had lost the initiative. Nevertheless, his main objective was to keep the U-boat campaign going long enough for new high-powered submarines, which could reach 30 knots, to enter the war. Fortunately for the Allies, labour shortages, design faults and air raids on German factories delayed production. The U-boat, however, remained a constant threat. Churchill wrote later of this Battle of the Atlantic: 'The only thing that ever really frightened me during the war was the U-boat peril.'

50%–59%			60%–69%		70%–79%	83%
achen	Essen	Munich	Bremen	Hanover	Bremerhaven	Bochum (Rühr)
ortmund	Frankfurt	Nuremberg	Cologne	Kassel	Hamburg	Bonn
resden	Koblenz	Stettin	Düsseldorf	Mainz		
mden			Hagen (Rühr)	Munster		

ercentage of area destroyed in individual German cities

Mass bombing

As the Axis powers hoped to break the morale of British civilians by blockade at sea, the Allies hoped to break the morale of German civilians by bombing from the air. Early in the war, Britain confined bombing to *military* targets, but such daylight 'precision bombing' was found not to be precise enough. Estimates showed that only one bomber in ten dropped its bombs within 8km of the target. The next strategy was to bomb at night. With the help of moonlight, larger areas such as rail centres were targeted.

In June 1941 when Germany invaded Russia, and again in 1942 when the assault on Stalingrad began, bombing over German cities was intensified to draw the Luftwaffe away from the Eastern Front and to disrupt munitions production and communication systems.

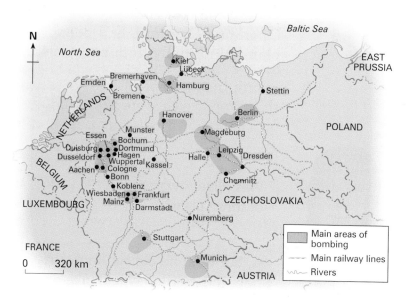

▲ The Allied bombing of Germany

THE ATTACK EGINS IN THE FACTORY

▲ A British propaganda poster congratulating workers contributing to the war effort

A new leader of Bomber Command, Air Marshal Sir Arthur 'Bomber' Harris, who was appointed in February 1942, favoured 'area bombing' rather than the destruction of specific targets. In May 1942, instead of the usual 250–350 bomber raids, he ordered the first 'thousand bomber' raid on Cologne. From this time, civilian areas became the main targets and military successes were regarded as bonuses. When the Americans began daylight bombing of Germany from August 1942, the Allies worked together to provide round-the-clock bombing.

Was the morale of the German citizens broken by the devastation this bombing must have caused?

Their morale remained high and war production was not halted. However then, in March 1944, bombing of German industry was stepped up considerably. The Allies were preparing for an invasion of France.

Allied air force: 10,000 combat aircraft, 2,000 transports	German air force: 300 machines (all types)	Allied navy – invasion coast: 7 battleships, 2 monitors, 23 cruisers, 77 destroyers	Allied navy – North Sea: 3 battleships, 3 carriers, 7 cruisers, 10 destroyers	German navy – North Sea: 3 cruisers, few destroyers

1944 June 6

THE END OF THE THIRD REICH

28

Overlord and D-Day

The invasion of France, codenamed Operation Overlord, had been planned formally from early 1943.

Was Hitler aware of these plans?

Yes, but what he did *not* know was where the invasion would take place. His commander in the West, von Runstedt, anticipated landings in the Pas-de-Calais region, whereas Rommel thought Normandy more likely.

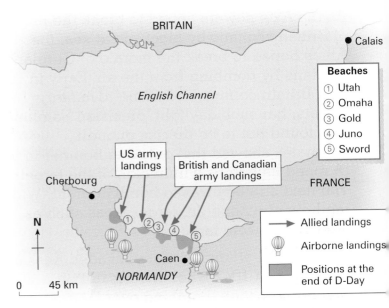

▲ The D-Day landings, Normandy, June 6, 1944

The Allies, had, in fact, decided on Normandy, but put in place elaborate deception plans that led Hitler into dividing his troops between the two areas. Part of this deception involved the establishment of a non-existent army in East Anglia. Wireless messages to General Montgomery's headquarters were routed through it and German agents, now working as 'double-agents' for Britain, sent false messages. Allied plans for the actual invasion were thorough and ingenious too. New equipment was made. Two artificial harbours (Mulberries) as large as medium-sized ports were made in sections ready to tow across the Channel. Twenty oil pipelines under the ocean (Pluto) were laid. Tracked vehicles were adapted. Some had flails to clear minefields, some could destroy concrete, some bridged dikes and others laid carpets down on the sands. D-Day itself, planned for June 5, had to be postponed because of a storm. The supreme commander of the Allied forces, General Eisenhower, so as not to miss the tide by a month, launched the attack at 2am on June 6, 1944. Luckily for the Allies, the worst of the storm had passed over. Around 20,000 airborne troops were dropped some kilometres inland. By 6am, 70,000 Allied soldiers were spread out along the five chosen beaches.

▲ Part of a Mulberry harbour carrying war provisions and trucks

156,000 Allied troops land on D-Day	Allies take Cherbourg	Allies take Caen	Falaise: 10,000 Germans died, 50,000 taken prisoner	Paris liberated	Operation Market Garden, Arnhem: 1,200 British died, 3,000 taken prisoner	Battle of the Bulge, Ardennes	German counter-attack halted
1944 June 6	June 26	July 19	July	August 25	September 17	December 16	1945 January

From Normandy to the Rhine

Was Allied progress rapid once troops were ashore?

Not always. The Germans were seasoned and determined fighters. The Americans suffered 3,000 casualties on Omaha Beach; and the British, expecting to take Caen on the first day, failed to reach it.

A storm lasting from June 18–22 hampered progress, destroying a Mulberry harbour with the loss of vehicles and stores. Then, after fierce fighting, Cherbourg was eventually captured on June 26 and Caen on July 19. The French Resistance managed to take Brittany, except for the ports. The Allies next broke the German line on July 20, but at the Falaise 'pocket' thousands of Germans escaped before the gap was closed. Those trapped at Falaise refused to surrender, thus holding back the whole Allied advance. Only after house-to-house fighting were the Germans defeated there.

Now Normandy was taken, the Allies – over a million and a half men strong, with fresh American troops landing in the south of France – advanced rapidly. Paris was liberated on August 25, 1944 and, by September, the whole of northern France, Belgium and Luxembourg were in Allied hands.

That month at Arnhem in Holland, the Allies, hoping to end the war quickly, tried to capture a bridge across the River Rhine and advance into Germany. The attempt failed and in December Hitler launched a surprise counter-attack in the Ardennes in southern Belgium (the Battle of the Bulge). Allied air attacks and superiority in numbers, despite early enemy successes, eventually halted the German offensive in January 1945.

▲ The first Allied landings on D-Day, June 6, 1944

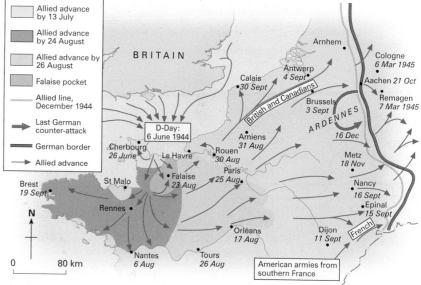

▲ Allied advance, June 1944 to March 1945

139

V weapons ('vergeltung' means retribution)	V1 flying bomb: 2,419 hit London, 3,132 hit other areas, 6,184 civilians killed	V2 long-range rocket: 517 hit London, 537 hit other areas, 2,754 civilians killed	V3 long-range gun: 25 barrels each, 127 metres long embedded in concrete and limestone, destroyed before use
1944 June	June 13, 1944 to March 1945	September 8, 1944 to March 1945	

Secret weapons

Weren't U-boats and the Luftwaffe used during the Normandy landings?

When six U-boats were sunk in the first few days of the invasion, and more damaged, the remainder were withdrawn from the conflict.

The Luftwaffe faced a severe shortage of fuel. Allied bombings had seriously affected their supplies of synthetic oil and, by September 1944, when a monthly minimum of 160,000 tonnes of fuel was needed, they were down to an allowance of 10,000 tonnes.

Hitler, however, now had secret V weapons, which he believed would assure victory for Germany. The V1 was a jet-propelled pilotless aircraft that first crossed the Channel from France on June 13, 1944. It had a warhead of one tonne of explosive and could reach 750kph. Nevertheless, as these bombs flew a set course and were clearly visible, they could in fact be intercepted. By August 1944 – with the aid of advanced radar, improved predictors and shells with proximity fuses – 80 per cent were being shot down from the ground.

▲ An unexploded V1 'doodlebug' bomb

The V2 launched in September was a long-range rocket, also with a warhead of about one tonne of explosive. Fired from Holland, capable of reaching 5,800kph and arriving without warning, it was impossible to intercept. The Allies, however, had some success with fighter-bomber attacks on the launch pads of these missiles.

The V3 was a long-range gun with 25 barrels and was intended to fire one shell on London every 12 seconds. Fortunately, Allied bomber attacks destroyed the V3 base near Calais before the gun could be used. Had these dangerous weapons been introduced earlier, the course of the war may well have been affected.

...ed ...mmer ...ensive ...taly	Rome captured	Russian summer offensive in White Russia	Warsaw rising: German victory	Romania signs armistice	Bulgaria signs armistice	Russians enter Belgrade in Yugloslavia	Russians retake Warsaw in Poland	Russians take Budapest in Hungary

...4 June		August	September			October	1945 January	February 12

Germany threatened

As it was, the Allies were closing in on Germany, not only from the west of Europe but from the east and south too. In Italy an Allied summer offensive was launched in June 1944, just before D-Day. Troops secured a beachhead at Anzio taken by the Germans in January that year, and, after heavy fighting, captured Rome. Although Hitler always opposed retreat, the Germans were forced to withdraw and consolidate a line further north.

The Germans also had to retreat when the Russians launched a successful offensive in June 1944 against their army in White Russia. By this time the Russians had a superiority of 8 to 1 in aircraft and 10 to 1 in tanks.

How did they achieve this?

Their war production, helped by 'new' factories in the east, far outstripped Germany's.

▲ Germany threatened, 1944–1945

From 1943 Russian annual production of armoured vehicles was around 30,000. German production of these reached a peak of 19,000 in 1944. This played no small part in helping the Russian advance through Poland, Romania, Bulgaria, Yugoslavia and Hungary, whose capital, Budapest, was taken on February 12, 1945.

Meanwhile, in the West, to help the Russian advance, hasten the collapse of German morale and shorten the war, 'Bomber' Harris ordered over a thousand bombers to attack Dresden, a vital communications centre. The city, regarded as architecturally splendid, was, by chance, packed with refugees fleeing from the Russians. In three short raids on February 13 and 14, it was estimated that over 130,000 people were killed. Industrial targets, though, were barely hit, and the railway lines were put out of action for only four days. The decision to launch this raid has been a subject of controversy ever since, many viewing it as an unnecessary raid.

Victory in Europe

On the Western Front on March 7, 1945, the Allies secured a bridgehead across the Rhine at Remagen. By March 25 seven Allied armies had crossed the Rhine over this and various swiftly built bridges and then moved against increasingly demoralised German armies.

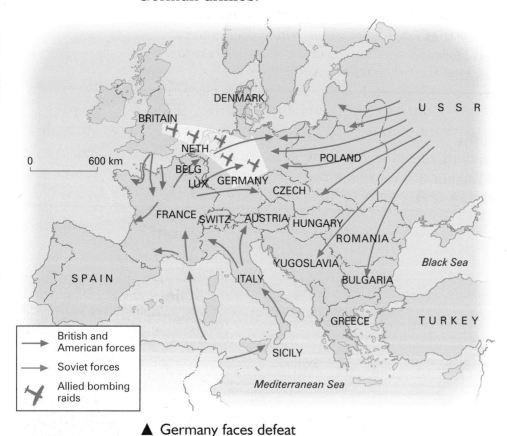

▲ Germany faces defeat

Still commanding those armies was Hitler, who had moved to an underground bunker in Berlin by late 1944. The Russians launched their attack on Berlin on April 16, 1945. As the city was bombarded from the air and from the ground, the SS, the Gestapo and the Hitler Youth – supported by a Home Guard of conscripted available men aged between 16 and 60 – fought street by street to save it. On April 29 Hitler was informed of the German unconditional surrender on the Italian Front and of the death of Mussolini, killed by Italian communist partisans the day before. By now Hitler had accepted the inevitability of defeat, and, on that same day, wrote his last will and political testament.

Did he express any remorse for his actions?

Hitler remained unrepentant and sought to blame the German officer corps for all that had gone wrong.

He placed most of the blame, however, on the Jews, 'the real guilty party in this murderous struggle' and who 'will be saddled with responsibility for it'. Then, on April 30, 1945 Hitler and his wife Eva Braun committed suicide. On May 7 representatives of all three of the Reich's fighting services surrendered unconditionally to the Western and Russian commands. The Third Reich, which Hitler had boasted would last a thousand years, had ended after just 12.

Kingdom of the Night

As the Allies advanced from east and west towards Berlin, liberating troops were able to enter the extermination camps across German-occupied Europe. Even the most battle-hardened of men were unprepared for the scenes that awaited them. The shock of the overwhelming stench of death, and the sight of thousands and thousands of the dead and barely living, were more than some could bear. At Belsen, the hair of some rescuers was reported to have turned white. At Dachau, rescuing American soldiers killed 300 SS guards and those inmates with enough strength and need for revenge killed 200 more. At some camps Allied soldiers forced the local German population to file past the unburied bodies, the crematoria and the torture rooms. At other camps, guards had destroyed buildings and burned records before the Allies entered, but ample evidence remained.

As photographs and reports were published, an incredulous world was forced to confront the enormity of this evil which existed. A new word, genocide – meaning the deliberate extermination of a race or people – entered the vocabulary. One survivor of Buchenwald, Elie Wiesel, later wrote: 'You were the liberators, but we, the diseased, emaciated, barely human survivors were your teachers. We taught you to understand the Kingdom of the Night.'

This kingdom of no boundaries had embraced about six million Jews, prisoners of war, priests, gypsies, Resistance workers, German opponents of Nazism, Jehovah's Witnesses, tramps, the mentally handicapped and chronically sick. This had been a Nazi 'kingdom' and, like the Nazi Empire, ended with the death of Hitler and victory for the Allies.

▲ Some of the 35,000 unburied dead at Bergen-Belsen. Approximately 40,000 prisoners were freed by British troops.

143

Battle of Philippine Sea: capture of Saigon by USA	US forces combine at Battle of Leyte, biggest naval battle of Second World War: US victory	Iwo Jima: took USA 6 weeks to conquer island 8km x 4km	Invasion of Okinawa by USA	Mass suicide attacks
1944 June 15	October 20	1945 February 19	1945 April to June	

THE END OF THE SECOND WORLD WAR

29

Bushido and kamikaze

In South-East Asia, where war continued, prisoners of war could not be liberated. Those captured by the Japanese – whether Allied soldiers or Burmese, Chinese, Indian or Filipino citizens – were brutally treated. If not killed immediately, sometimes by decapitation, they were placed in prison and labour camps where disease, starvation and unrelenting ill-treatment caused thousands to die.

For the Japanese soldiers themselves, capture in battle – according to their warrior code of bushido – was a dishonour. Men would fight to the death, even swim out to sea to avoid capture. In one battle, fought in New Guinea, out of 13,000 Japanese put out of action, only 38 were taken prisoner. The Pacific campaign remained chiefly one for the Americans, and, by adopting an 'island hopping' strategy, they retook the ferociously defended islands step by step, one by one. By June 1944, having taken Saigon Island, the Americans were poised to bomb Tokyo itself. Other victories, the capture of Tinian and Guam Islands, followed.

▲ A kamikaze attack damages an aircraft carrier in April 1945

The Japanese, now facing defeat, adopted a new tactic. From October, in the Battle of Leyte, Japanese pilots volunteered for kamikaze (divine wind) suicide missions. Over 5,000 flew their planes, which were packed with explosives, into enemy ships. With no return journey to consider, fuel lasted twice the usual range so Allied targets well out to sea could be struck.

Did this tactic succeed?

Although 36 ships were eventually sunk and the missions were much feared by US naval crews, the Japanese could not, at this stage of the war, threaten American superiority.

Furthermore, although scientists in Japan had hoped to develop an atomic bomb in time to influence the outcome of the war, in November 1944 they concluded that, for their part, this was not possible.

No surrender

By February 1945 the American General MacArthur had retaken the Philippine Islands and plans for an Allied invasion of Japan were established.

Did the Japanese consider surrender?

Despite having lost 88 per cent of her merchant fleet and 80 per cent of her oil supplies, surrender was not contemplated by the powerful military generals.

The battles that followed for the islands of Iwo Jima in February and Okinawa in April were particularly hard-fought victories for the Americans. At Okinawa they faced mass kamikaze attacks, which succeeded in sinking 25 ships in one day. Even a kamikaze battleship was sent on a one-way journey to create havoc there. It was sunk before arrival. The island was eventually taken on June 21.

▲ War in the Pacific, 1942–1945

By June Tokyo and several other Japanese cities were being severely damaged by intensive bombing attacks and the Americans' invasion date was now set for November. Emperor Hirohito, realising what Japan would face, sought diplomatic means to end the war. When, however, it became clear that the Japanese would not accept unconditional surrender, invasion plans continued. The Japanese prepared by designing new suicide weapons. These included a torpedo to which a man would be strapped to guide it to its target. But there was no chance of using these in battle. Scientists in the USA had by now developed an atomic bomb in time to influence the outcome of the war. After a successful testing of this bomb, the new American President, Harry S Truman, with Churchill's knowledge, gave the order to use it against the Japanese.

Atomic bomb tested in New Mexico, USA	All plant and animal life killed within 3.2km radius	Atomic bomb (uranium) dropped on Hiroshima	Russia declares war on Japan	Atomic bomb (plutonium) dropped on Nagasaki	Formal surrender of Japan: VJ (Victory in Japan) Day	End of Second World War
1945 July 16		August 6	August 8	August 9	September 2	

The end of the Second World War

How powerful was the atom bomb?

Imagine, if you can, 2,000 bombers of that period dropping all their bombs at the same time and this gives you some idea of the explosive power of a single atom bomb.

Unlike 'conventional' bombs, though, atomic explosions also produce radiation, which causes sickness and death for many years afterwards. The first of the three bombs made was used in the successful test in the desert of New Mexico on July 16, 1945. The second bomb was dropped on the Japanese city of Hiroshima on August 6, causing 92,233 deaths within two weeks. Various effects reported included:

- a blinding flash of light.
- intense suffocating heat that incinerated nearby human beings so that nothing remained except their shadows, burned into pavements.
- a wind-blast from the 'fireball' reaching 800kph.
- black raindrops as big as marbles.
- survivors within a 3km radius with burned, peeled and melted skin.

▲ 'A mushroom of boiling dust' over Nagasaki

On August 9 the third bomb was dropped, this time on Nagasaki. Over 40,000 people were killed and 5,000 died in the following three months. On August 14 the Japanese agreed to unconditional surrender, though they requested that the Emperor's position should be preserved. The formal surrender of Japan, in fact, took place on September 2, 1945.

Taking the German invasion of Poland on September 1, 1939 as the beginning of the Second World War, the conflict had lasted precisely six years. The explosion of the atom bombs marked the end of this war and was to change the nature of warfare forever.

▲ The city of Hiroshima after the bomb

146

The United Nations

Despite the perceived failure of the League of Nations, the 'Big Three' (Churchill, Roosevelt and Stalin) at the Teheran Conference of 1943 agreed to set up after the war a new international peace-keeping organisation, the United Nations. After further discussions at the Yalta Conference in February 1945, the organisation came into being in June that year.

Security Council Can order ceasefires, economic sanctions and use of force. Members must obey decisions. 5 permanent members (USA, USSR, UK, France and China) and 10 temporary members.

International Court of Justice 15 judges advise on legal matters.

Secretariat International Civil Service. Runs UN. Headed by Secretary-General.

UN Peace-keeping Forces Troops from all member countries.

Trusteeship Council In charge of territories under UN control or mandate.

Specialised Agencies include:
- UNESCO (UN Educational Scientific and Cultural Organisation).
- UNICEF (UN Children's Fund).
- WHO (World Health Organisation).
- World Bank.

General Assembly Each member has one vote. On important decisions, two-thirds majority needed.

Specialised Agencies include:
- FAO (Food and Agricultural Organisation).
- GATT (General Agreement on Tariffs and Trade).
- ILO (International Labour Organisation).
- IMF (International Monetary Fund).

Economic and Social Council 54 members. Coordinates specialised agencies. Concerns itself with certain matters, e.g. human rights.

In 1948 the General Assembly gave its approval to the Universal Declaration of Human Rights. Article I begins:

> All human beings are born free and equal in dignity and rights. They are endowed with reason and conscience and should act towards one another in a spirit of brotherhood.

This vision of hope, a world at peace, was by then already being put to the test as the UN found itself caught between two 'superpowers' which were battling for supremacy in a 'new' war.

Germany to be divided into 4 zones: American, British, French and Soviet. Berlin similarly divided.	War criminals brought to trial	Eastern Europe under 'Soviet sphere of influence'	Free elections for liberated countries	'Big Three' agree to join United Nations

1945 Yalta Conference

Towards Cold War

At the Yalta Conference of February 1945, the 'Big Three', despite Roosevelt's and Churchill's distrust of communism, were able to negotiate over most terms. The major disagreement concerned Poland. Stalin wanted the border of the USSR to move west into Poland which, in turn, would move *its* border west into Germany.

Churchill persuaded Roosevelt to accept this if, in return, the USSR did not interfere in Greece, where Britain was trying to prevent communism from taking over. Stalin agreed to this.

At the Potsdam Conference of July 1945, when war in Europe was over, a changed 'Big Three' faced a changed situation. Stalin by then had not withdrawn his troops from the liberated countries, so he effectively remained in control of Finland, Poland, Czechoslovakia, Bulgaria, Romania and the Baltic States. Despite Allied protests, he set up a communist government in Poland.

▲ Attlee, Truman and Stalin (all seated) meet at Potsdam in July 1945

Roosevelt had died in April, and the new US President, Harry Truman, who was strongly anti-communist, was prepared to take a stance against Stalin. Halfway through the conference, Churchill lost the election in Britain, and was replaced by a new Prime Minister, Clement Attlee. With Churchill gone, the suspicions and rivalry between Truman and Stalin surfaced. They disagreed over what to do with Germany and the amount of reparation that should be paid. Stalin demanded compensation but Truman, wanting to avoid the mistakes at Versailles in 1919, resisted. They also disagreed over Stalin's policy in Eastern Europe and no satisfactory conclusions were reached.

Truman's suspicions over Stalin's intentions were, in fact, to be realised. By 1946 Hungary, Romania, Bulgaria and Albania all had communist governments too.

...astern sector ... Germany ...der USSR ...ontrol	Albania becomes communist	Bulgaria has communist coalition; members execute leaders of other parties	Romania elects communist prime minister	Yugoslavia: President Tito applies communism in own way	Poland: communists force non-communist leader into exile	Hungary: communists largest single party	Czechoslovakia: one-party communist state
...945–1949	1945	1945	1945	1945	1947	1947	1948

The Iron Curtain

In 1946 Churchill, in a landmark speech, described the border that separated the Soviet-controlled communist countries of Eastern Europe from the capitalist democracies of the West as an 'Iron Curtain'. This curtain, a symbol of division, was to remain lowered for nearly 50 years.

As Stalin tightened control over the communist countries, Truman was determined to 'contain' communism and prevent it from spreading. Every action by the USSR regarded as challenging the West was met with a response by the USA.

At the same time, both sides increased spending on weapons. An 'arms race', in which each tried to outdo the other and which included nuclear weapons, developed. It was these two powers – not Britain or France, which were no longer rich enough or big enough to compete – that became recognised as the world's 'superpowers', with both jostling for supremacy. As tensions between them grew, with both openly denouncing each other's policies and hurling insults back and forth, people began to talk of a Cold War.

What is that?

A Cold War, as distinct from one fought in the 'heat of battle', is a war of words and propaganda. Though these two 'superpowers' never faced each other in a 'hot' war, many confrontations around the world connected with the Cold War did become real wars.

149

Origins in Russian Revolution	and Russian civil war	USSR military alliance with Germany; Stalin distrusted by Allies	Stalin expected more support from Allies during Second World War	Potsdam disagreements	Soviet domination of Eastern Europe	Churchill's speech: Iron Curtain — Communist East / Democrat West	Marshall Aid Plan: USA to help shattered economies of Europe
1917	1918–1921	1939	1939–1945	1945 July	1945–1948	1946 March	1947 June

Stalin forbids communist countries to apply for Marshall Aid	First Cominform coordinates work of communist party in Eastern Europe	Soviet blockade of Berlin	NATO military alliance of Western powers	China becomes communist	USA intervenes in Korean Civil War: communist North versus anti-communist South – military stalemate	Senator Joe McCarthy leads anti-communist crusade in USA
1947	1947 October	1948–1949	1949	1949 October	1950–1953	1950–1954

FLASHPOINT   FLASHPOINT

Death of Stalin	Korean War armistice	Khruschev becomes Soviet leader, de-Stalinisation, end of Cominform, peaceful co-existence	Warsaw Pact: military alliance between USSR and Eastern Europe	Protests in Poland: Red Army restores order	Hungarian anti-communist uprising crushed	Communists build Berlin Wall	Cuban Missile Crisis
1953	1953	1953	1955	1956	1956 October	1961 August	1962 October

FLASHPOINT

Hotline between Kremlin and White House A/W 31e	Main USA involvement in Vietnam: communist North versus anti-communist South	'Domino' Theory 	Prague 'Spring': fresh ideas in Czechoslovakia, leader Dubček removed from power	Détente (relaxation). Summit meetings. Money diverted to help poor. Improved relations between USA and China.
1962	1963–1973		1968	1970s

End of Vietnam War: defeat and withdrawal of USA	American astronauts and Soviet cosmonauts shake hands in space	High point of détente 	Founding of Polish trade union, Solidarity	Collapse of communism in Eastern Europe	Berlin Wall dismantled	US President George Bush and Soviet leader Mikhail Gorbachev declare Cold War over
1975			1980 August	1989 May to 1990 March	1989 November	1989 December

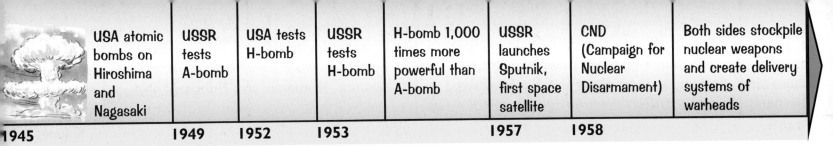

	USA atomic bombs on Hiroshima and Nagasaki	USSR tests A-bomb	USA tests H-bomb	USSR tests H-bomb	H-bomb 1,000 times more powerful than A-bomb	USSR launches Sputnik, first space satellite	CND (Campaign for Nuclear Disarmament)	Both sides stockpile nuclear weapons and create delivery systems of warheads
1945		1949	1952	1953		1957	1958	

The arms race: nuclear weapons

Nuclear warheads fitted to missiles or carried by bombers	ICBMs (Inter-Continental Ballistic Missiles): long-range missiles	SLBMs (Submarine-Launched Ballistic Missiles): launched under sea anywhere in world	MIRVs (Multiple Independently Targeted Re-entry Vehicles): up to 10 warheads launched at different targets	USA 1054	Nuclear missiles	USSR 1050

1960s–1970s Main nuclear weapons   1969

Disarmament attempts	Partial Test-Ban Treaty: over 100 nations sign, all nuclear test explosions, except those underground, banned	Non-Proliferation Treaty: over 100 nations sign, those without nuclear weapons agree not to make them	Strategic Arms Limitation Talks (USA and USSR)	SALT 1 long-range weapon limits SALT 2

1960s–1970s   1963   1968   1972   1979

	Warheads	USSR 7000	Pershing II: USA intermediate-range nuclear warhead	Strategic Defence Initiative (USA): space-based laser systems destroy missiles before they reach their targets ('Star Wars')

1981   1983

Reagan and Gorbachev nearly reach agreement on nuclear weapon reduction, Reagan refuses to give up 'Star Wars'	INF (Intermediate Nuclear Forces Treaty): land-based INF weapons with range of 500–5,000km destroyed (including Pershing II)	START (Strategic Arms Reduction Treaty): reduces long-range nuclear weapons by a third

1986   1987   1991

The Berlin Blockade

As Berlin lay 160km inside the Soviet zone of Germany, the Allies had to send supplies to their Berlin zones through the Soviet zone. In 1946 the Allies, to help rebuild the German economy, combined their Berlin zones. In 1948, to facilitate trade, they introduced a new currency for use in these zones. Stalin, wanting Berlin to be dependent on the USSR and not the Allies, decided to force the Allies out. In June 1948 he sent in tanks and cut all road, rail and canal supply links to it from West Germany.

▲ The four zones of Germany and the four zones of Berlin

Did the Allies send in tanks to forcefully dismantle the road and rail blocks?

No, as this might have been interpreted as an act of 'hot' war. Instead, supplies to the two million Berliners, who were now cut off, were airlifted in.

There were fears that the planes might be shot down but, in fact, no shots were fired. The Soviets, too, backed away from 'hot' war. At the height of the crisis – when war was a distinct possibility – the Allies formed a military alliance (NATO) with other Western powers in case of armed attack from unnamed aggressors. The airlift, in which planes carrying supplies from West German air bases landed every three minutes night and day for over ten months, was surprisingly successful, and on May 12, 1949 Stalin lifted the blockade. Eleven days later the Allied zones became the Federal Republic of Germany (FDR) – West Germany. In October 1949 the Soviet zone became the German Democratic Republic (GDR) – East Germany.

The Berlin Wall

After 1949 the Allies still controlled West Berlin and, by 1961, over two million East Berliners, many well-qualified and skilled workers, had defected to the West.

Why?

American aid had transformed West Berlin into a showpiece of capitalism where workers enjoyed better working conditions and a choice of luxury goods. In contrast, those in East Berlin worked long hours, had a limited choice of things to buy and endured food shortages.

The presence of a prosperous democratic city in the middle of an Iron Curtain country was an embarrassment to the USSR. In 1959 and 1961 the Soviet leader, Khruschev, proposed that the occupying powers should leave Berlin. The Allies refused. The East German government, with Khruschev's approval, took action.

Again, the war remained a 'cold' one rather than a 'hot' one. The wall stayed up, but the Allies held firm in West Berlin. The Iron Curtain had been an imaginary symbol of division. The Berlin Wall was an *actual* symbol of division – of Germany, of Europe, of the communist East and the democratic West.

153

USA helps Cuba become independent from Spain	USA had naval and air base at Guantanamo on Cuba	USA controlled 90% of Cuban mines, 90% of cattle ranches, 4% of sugar industry	Overthrow of Batista by communist Fidel Castro	Trade pact with Soviets	Diplomatic relations between Cuba and USA cut off	Bay of Pigs
1898			1959	1960 February	1961	1961 April 17

The Cuban Missile Crisis

Cuba, a Caribbean island 150km from Florida, south-eastern USA, had been a long-time ally of the USA, but in 1959 the American-backed dictator Batista was overthrown by Fidel Castro, a left-wing revolutionary. When Castro instituted reforms such as taking over American-owned businesses and seizing land to redistribute to peasants, these actions were regarded by the USA as those of a communist. When Castro visited the USA in 1959, President Eisenhower was 'too busy' to meet him. The USA cut off economic aid and refused to buy Cuban sugar, the backbone of the Cuban economy. Eisenhower, fearing the spread of communism elsewhere in Latin America, ordered the US Central Intelligence Agency (CIA) to prepare plans for the overthrow of Castro.

As diplomatic relations between Cuba and the USA deteriorated, those between Cuba and the USSR grew friendlier. Khruschev offered to buy Cuban sugar and sent in arms. In 1960 the new American President, John F Kennedy, inherited Eisenhower's plans and was advised by the CIA that US landings in Cuba would trigger a popular uprising against Castro. On April 17, 1961, Kennedy authorised an invasion by a force of 1,400 men, mainly Cuban exiles trained by the CIA.

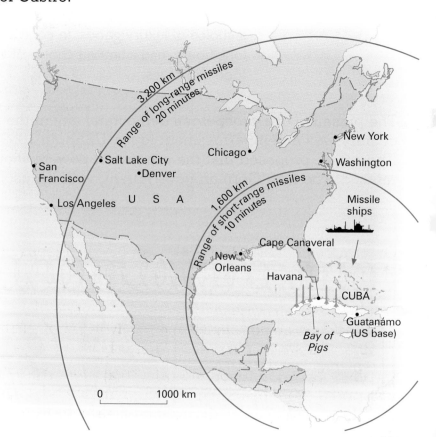

▲ The location and range of nuclear missiles on Cuba by mid 1962

Was it successful?

No, it was a fiasco. Within three days of landing at the Bay of Pigs, most of the men had been captured or killed. There was no sign of an uprising.

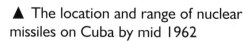

For Kennedy it was a humiliation. For Castro it was a great propaganda victory. For Khruschev it was a chance to wield more influence. Cuba's armed forces were now flooded with Russian jet bombers, jet fighters, tanks, radar vans, 5,000 Soviet technicians – and then nuclear missiles.

Both USSR and USA had hundreds of missiles pointed at each other from their respective countries	Both sides could destroy the human and animal world several times over	USA short-range missiles in NATO countries could hit USSR in minutes; long-range missiles (ICBMs) based in USA would take about 30 minutes

96 I

Nuclear war?

Kennedy, aware of the build-up of conventional weapons on the island, had warned the Soviets on September 11, 1962 that he would prevent by whatever means might be necessary 'Cuba becoming an offensive military base' – which clearly meant a nuclear-missile base.

▲ Photographic evidence of the medium-range ballistic missile base in Cuba, 1962

Were the Soviets acting illegally?

No. The USA already had nuclear missiles based in Turkey and NATO countries (including nuclear warheads in Britain) aimed at the USSR.

On October 14, 1962 two American U2 spy planes brought back photographs showing 10 medium-range missiles spread over various sites on Cuba, already angled on mobile launchers and pointed at the US mainland. These were capable of carrying nuclear warheads and had a range of over 1,600km. Other photographs showed sites being prepared to receive longer-range missiles and some showed bombers capable of carrying nuclear bombs being uncrated.

Intelligence reports then indicated that more than 25 Soviet ships with more missile equipment were heading across the Atlantic for Cuba. Kennedy and his advisers now faced a serious crisis indeed. Their options included:

1 Doing nothing.

2 Protesting through diplomatic means.

3 Placing a naval blockade around Cuba.

4 Launching a selected air attack to destroy the nuclear bases.

5 Launching an all-out invasion of Cuba by air and sea.

On October 22, 1962 Kennedy appeared on television. Reaching a worldwide audience, he announced his decision to place an 800km blockade around Cuba. He called on Khruschev 'to halt and eliminate this reckless and provocative threat to world peace... He has the opportunity now to move the world back from the abyss of destruction'.

Consequences of Cuban Crisis	Hotline between Kremlin and White House	Nuclear Test-Ban Treaty forbade tests in atmosphere	Kennedy's reputation greatly enhanced	Cuba was never invaded	Cuba still communist, Castro still in power

1962   1963   2000

Back from the abyss

1962	
Tuesday, October 23	Warning from Moscow – blockade will be ignored.
Wednesday, October 24	Blockade comes into effect. Soviet missile-carrying ships, accompanied by Soviet submarines, approach 800km blockade zone. 10.32am: The 20 ships closest to the zone alter course and abandon Cuban destinations.
Thursday, October 25	Photographs reveal work on missile sites is continuing.
Friday, October 26	Kennedy receives personal letter from Khruschev, who offers to withdraw missiles if USA agrees to lift blockade and never to invade Cuba. These terms are acceptable to Kennedy.
Saturday, October 27	Kennedy receives a second letter from Khruschev. This revises the proposals of the first and demands withdrawal of US missiles from Turkey. Kennedy rejects these terms. A US U2 spy plane is shot down over Cuba and the pilot killed. Kennedy does not know whether this has been authorised by Khruschev or not. As tension heightens, Kennedy is advised to launch an immediate reprisal attack on Cuba. He delays this action by replying to Khruschev's first letter of October 26 and ignoring the second. He says that Khruschev's terms are 'generally acceptable' but, if the USSR does not withdraw immediately, it 'would surely lead to an intensification of the crisis and a grave risk to the peace of the world'.
Sunday, October 28	Khruschev agrees to remove all Russian missiles, bombers and troops from Cuba. Kennedy privately agrees to remove nuclear missiles from Turkey.

The crisis was over. Having brought the world to the brink of a nuclear war, both sides realised they had to step back or fall into the 'abyss of destruction' – such would be the impact nuclear war would have upon civilisation.

Hungarians dismantle barbed-wire fence at border with Austria	Poland: free elections bring in non-communist leader	Events in East Germany lead to dismantling of Berlin Wall	Czech government opens borders with West	Bulgarians demonstrate against communists	Romania: execution of communist dictator Ceausescu	Latvia leads Baltic States by declaring independence from USSR
1989 May	June	September to November	November	December	December	1990 March

The collapse of communism

In 1985 the new Soviet leader, Mikhail Gorbachev, wanting to preserve communism but recognising the Soviet economy was approaching bankruptcy, undertook a series of reforms. Central to his programme were the twin policies of 'perestroika' (economic restructuring) and 'glasnost' (more open government).

Part of the economic reforms involved cuts in defence spending, and it was Gorbachev who took the initiative towards ending the arms race by proposing arms limitation talks with the USA. His policy of 'glasnost', which encouraged a more democratic society, had a tremendous impact on communist-controlled countries.

In December 1988, during a speech to the UN, Gorbachev made it clear that the use or threat of force was no longer part of Soviet policy. Statements such as these triggered an amazing sequence of events the year after in Eastern Europe, which signalled the end of communism.

▲ Dismantling the Berlin Wall

East Germany was central to this collapse. In September 1989 thousands of East Germans on holiday in Hungary and Czechoslovakia refused to return home and escaped to West Germany through Austria. In November, when Gorbachev visited East Germany, there were huge demonstrations demanding freedom in many cities. The East German leader, Honeker, ordered troops to fire on demonstrators. They refused, and Gorbachev declined to send in tanks to restore order.

In December, as thousands of East Germans marched to checkpoints at the Berlin Wall, the guards threw down their weapons and joined the crowds. The wall then began to be dismantled. Two years later, the USSR and its communist system collapsed and was replaced by a commonwealth of 15 independent states. The Iron Curtain, after casting a shadow for nearly 50 years, was lifted. Europe's frontiers were opened up again.

Kings and queens of Great Britain and Ireland

Name	Also known as	Age at succession	Family	Died	Buried
Victoria	Last of the Hanoverians Kingdom of Hanover passed to her uncle Ernest, Duke of Cumberland Proclaimed Empress of India, 1877	Age 18 as Queen of Great Britain and Ireland	Husband: Albert, Prince of Saxe-Coburg Gotha Children: Victoria, EDWARD, Alice, Alfred, Helena, Louise, Arthur, Leopold, Beatrice	January 22, Osborne, Isle of Wight Age 81 Of old age	Frogmore, Windsor
Born 1819		👑 1837		**Died 1901**	
Edward VII	The peace-maker First of the House of Saxe-Coburg Gotha	Age 59 as King of Great Britain and Ireland, and Emperor of India	Wife: Alexandra Children: Albert, GEORGE, Louise, Victoria, Maud, John	May 6, Buckingham Palace Age 68 Of pneumonia and a series of heart attacks	St George's Chapel, Windsor
Born 1841		👑 1901		**Died 1910**	
George V	Adopted family name of Windsor	Age 44 as King of Great Britain and Ireland, and Emperor of India	Wife: Princess Mary of Teck Children: EDWARD, GEORGE, Mary, Henry, George, John	January 20, Sandringham Age 70 Of pneumonia following general weakening	St George's Chapel, Windsor
Born 1865	1917	👑 1910		**Died 1936**	
Edward VIII		Age 41 as King of Great Britain, Ireland and the British Dominions beyond the seas, and Emperor of India Abdicated on December 11, 1936 after reigning for ten months	Wife: Mrs Wallace Simpson Children: None	May 28, Paris Age 78	Frogmore, Windsor
Born 1894		👑 1936		**Died 1972**	
George VI		Age 40 as King of Great Britain and Ireland and the British Dominions beyond the seas Discontinued the title of Emperor of India in 1947	Wife: Elizabeth Bowes-Lyon Children: ELIZABETH, Margaret	February 6, Sandringham Age 56 Of cancer	St George's Chapel, Windsor
Born 1895		👑 1936		**Died 1952**	
Elizabeth II		Age 25 as Queen of Great Britain and Northern Ireland and of her other Realms and Territories, and Head of the Commonwealth	Husband: Lieutenant Philip Mountbatten (Duke of Edinburgh) Children: Charles, Anne, Andrew, Edward		
Born 1926		👑 1952			

Index

Abyssinia (Ethiopia) 89, 104, 105
'air aces' 34
aircraft, early 11, 13, 14
aircraft carriers 125, 127, 144
airships 9, 13, 30, 34
Air Force, British/Royal 29, 34, 112–118, 136
Air Force, German (Luftwaffe) 104, 105, 107, 114–116, 121, 123, 128, 137, 138, 140
Alam el Halfa, Battle of 129
All Quiet on the Western Front 106
'Alphabet Agencies' 64, 65
Amiens, Battle of 39, 46, 47
Anderson shelters 117
Anschluss 106
Anti-Comintern Pact 89, 106, 107
anti-semitism 87–96
Anzac 29
appeasement 106, 108, 111
Armistice (of 1918) 47
arms race, nuclear 149, 151
army, British 9, 24–26, 29, 32, 34–40, 44, 45, 129
army, German 21, 24, 26, 35, 51, 52, 95, 101, 104, 107, 108, 110–112, 120–123, 128
Arnhem campaign 139
Aryan race idea 92, 96, 98, 100, 106, 108, 121, 131
astronauts/cosmonauts 150
Atlantic, Battle of the 134–136
atomic bomb 145, 146, 151
Attlee, Clement 148
Auschwitz extermination camp 110, 124, 131
Australia 29, 47, 116, 126, 127
Austria/Austria–Hungary 6, 21–23, 26, 28, 29, 47–49, 51, 53, 60, 75, 90, 106, 107, 157
autarky 101

Babi Yar 123
Bay of Pigs 154
Belgium/Belgian 23, 25–27, 47, 50, 51, 91, 112, 113, 116, 139
Belsen extermination camp 143
Berlin 89, 116, 142, 143, 148, 150, 152, 157
Berlin airlift and blockade 152
Berlin Wall 150, 153, 157
bicycles 12, 14
black Americans 60, 61, 66
Blackshirts 86, 87, 95
Blériot, Louis 14
Bletchley Park 134, 136
Blitz (on London) 116, 117, 120
Blitzkrieg 112, 121, 123
Bolsheviks (Reds) 70, 71, 74–79, 103
bombing (by Allies) of Germany 137, 140
Bonus Marchers 63
Brest-Litovsk, Treaty of 46, 76, 77
Britain/British 5–9, 11–15, 17, 21, 23–31, 33–35, 38–43, 45–50, 54–56, 60, 78, 86, 87, 104–122, 125–126, 129, 134–139, 143–145, 147–149, 152, 155, 158
Britain, Battle of 116, 117
British Expeditionary Force (BEF), First World War 25, 27, 35
British Expeditionary Force (BEF), Second World War 112
Brownshirts 95
Buchenwald extermination camp 97, 143
Bulge, Battle of the 139
Bush, George 150
bushido 144

Cable Street Riots 87
Cambrai offensive 40
Campbell-Bannerman 19
Canada, Canadian 9, 28, 29, 40, 44, 47, 59–61, 68, 109, 116, 119, 152

Caporetto, Battle of 28
car 11–13, 56–58, 61, 93
Capone, Al 59, 60
Castro, Fidel 154, 156
'Cat and Mouse Act' 20
cemeteries, military 48
Chamberlain, Neville 106, 107, 109, 111
Champagne, Battle of 27, 40
Cheka (secret police) 77, 78, 80, 85
Chelmo extermination camp 124
China/Chinese 105, 125, 126, 144, 147, 150
Churchill, Winston 20, 39, 111, 113, 114, 116, 117, 119, 133, 135, 136, 145, 147–150
cinema 8, 31, 57, 58, 88, 93, 102
City of Benares (liner) 109
civil war, Russian 78, 79
civil war, Spanish 105, 107
class system, Edwardian 7
Clemenceau, Georges 50, 52
codebreaking 134–136
Cold War 149, 150–157
collectivisation 80–82
Colossus Mark I computer 134
Cominform 150
communism/communist 70, 71, 76, 77, 79–87, 89, 91, 92, 94, 103, 104, 106, 108, 121, 122, 142, 148–150, 153, 154, 156, 157
Compiègne 47
concentration camps 95–97, 101, 103, 110, 124, 131, 143
convoy system 42, 46, 117, 135, 136
Coral Sea, Battle of 127
Coventry, bombing of 117
Crippen, Doctor 9, 10
Cuban Missile Crisis 150, 154–156
Curie, Marie and Pierre 15, 16, 17
Czechoslovakia/Czech 53, 78, 106–108, 116, 148–150, 152, 157

Dachau extermination camp 97, 131, 143
Danzig 51, 108
Dardanelles 29
D-Day 138, 139, 141
Defence of the Realm Act (DORA) 30
dekulakisation 81
Denmark/Danish 51, 61, 111, 113, 132
Depression, the Great 63, 64
Desert Rats (British 8th Army) 129, 130
disarmament 151
Doenitz, Admiral 135, 136
dogfights 34
Domino Theory 150
'Dopolavoro' 88
Dowding, Air Marshal 115
Dreadnoughts 21, 32
Dresden, bombing of 137, 141
Dual Alliance 6
Duma 72–74
Dunkirk, evacuation of 113

Edward VII 5–8, 19, 20, 158
Einstein, Albert 15
Eisenhower, General 138, 154
El Alamein, Battle of 129
Enabling Act 94
Enigma machine 134–136
Entente Cordiale 6
evacuation (from British cities) 109
extermination camps 124, 131, 143

Falaise 'pocket' 139
fascism/fascist 86–89, 103, 108, 130
fighter planes, First World War 34
Five Year Plans 82
'flappers' 58
force-feeding 19, 20

Ford, Henry 13, 60
Fourteen Points 49–51, 53
France/French 6–8, 11, 14, 15, 21–24, 26–29, 35, 40, 42, 44, 46–48, 50, 51, 54, 55, 61, 78, 91, 104–114, 116, 120, 125, 131, 132, 137–139, 147–149, 152
Franco, General 105
Franz Ferdinand, Archduke 22
Free French 132

Gallipoli 29
Gaulle, Charles de 132
GCHQ 134
George V 25, 30, 48, 158
George VI 113, 117, 158
Germany/German 5–7, 9, 11, 13, 21–24, 26–31, 33–35, 38–44, 46–55, 58, 60, 70, 73, 74, 77, 78, 87, 89, 90–116, 118, 120–126, 128–139, 143, 145–150, 152, 157
Gestapo 95, 101, 132, 142
'glasnost' 157
Goebbels, Joseph 93, 102
Gorbachev, Mikail 150, 157
Goering, Hermann 95, 115
Greece/Greek 28, 29, 53, 55, 61, 87, 120, 131, 132, 148
Guantanamo 154
Guernica, bombing of 105
gulags (labour camps) 82, 85

H-bomb 151
Haig, D, Field Marshal 43, 46, 47
Haile Selassie 105
Harris, Air Marshal 137, 141
Himmler 95
Hindenberg (German president) 93–95
Hirohito, Emperor 145–146
Hiroshima, A-bomb on 146, 151
Hitler, Adolf 90–96, 98–108, 111–114, 116, 120–124, 128, 129, 132, 138–143
Hitler Youth 99, 102, 142
Holland/Dutch 60, 61, 94, 112, 113, 125–127, 131, 139, 140
Hollywood 58, 106
Holocaust 122
Home Guard 114, 119
Honour and Gold Cross of German Mother 100
Hong Kong 126
Hoover, Herbert 61, 63
hotline (between USSR and USA) 150, 156
Human Rights, Universal Declaration of 147
Hungary/Hungarian 53, 61, 108, 131, 141, 148–150, 152, 157
Hurricane (air fighter) 115
hyperinflation, German 91

India/Indian 5, 25, 29, 126, 127, 144, 158
innovations, wartime 30
Iron Curtain 149, 153, 157
Italy/Italian 6, 9, 21, 26, 28, 48, 51, 54, 55, 58, 86–89, 105–107, 120, 125, 126, 129, 130, 134, 141, 142, 152
Iwo Jima, Battle of 144, 145

Japan/Japanese 10, 28, 54, 55, 72, 89, 105–107, 125–127, 134, 144–147
'Jazz Age' 58
Jews 53, 60, 87, 89, 91, 92, 96–98, 102, 103, 110, 122–124, 131, 132, 142, 143
Jutland, Battle of 33

Kaiser Wilhelm II 5, 6, 21, 26, 47, 52
kamikaze attacks 144, 145
Kennedy, John F 156–156
Kerensky 75, 76
Khruschev, Nikita 150, 153–156

'Kinder, Kirche, Küche' 118
Kitchener, Lord 25, 39
Korean War 150
Kristallnacht 97
Ku Klux Klan 60
Kulaks 81
Kursk, Battle of 130

labour camps, Nazi 100, 101
laissez-faire 57, 61, 63
Land Army, Women's 32, 33, 118
Lausanne, Treaty of 53
Lawrence, T E (of Arabia) 29
League of Nations 51, 53–56, 68, 104, 105, 125, 147
lebensraum (living space) 92, 108, 121
Lenin 71, 74–80, 84, 85
Leningrad 80, 121–123
Lenoir, Etienne 11
Leyte, Battle of 144
Lloyd George, David 39, 43, 47, 50
London 8, 9, 12, 14, 17, 18, 20, 30, 32, 44, 87, 107, 109, 116, 117, 140
Long, Huey 66
Ludendorff, Gerard 47
Lumière brothers 8
Lusitania (liner) 33

MacArthur, General 145
McCarthy, Joe 150
Maginot Line 112
Marconi, Guglielmo 9
Marne, Battle of the 27
Married Women's Property Act 17
Marshall Aid Plan 150
'mass' aspects of 20th century 7–10, 12, 13, 25, 56, 57, 100, 137
Masurian Lakes, Battle of the 28
Mein Kampf 92, 98
Mengele, Joseph 131
Mensheviks 70, 71, 74, 75, 78
Midway, Battle of 127
Mons, Battle of 27
Montgomery, B, General 129, 130, 138
Moroccan crises 21
Moscow 68, 76, 121–123, 128, 130, 156
Mosley, Sir Oswald 86, 88
Mudd, Private Jack 44, 45
Mulberry harbours 138, 139
Munich Conference 107
Munich Putsch 91, 92, 103, 115
Mussolini, Benito 55, 86–90, 105, 107, 120, 130, 142

'Nacht und Nabel' (Night and Fog) decree 124
Nagasaki, A-bomb on 146, 151
NATO 150, 152, 155
navy, British/Royal 5, 9, 21, 29, 30, 31, 33, 42, 104, 113, 136
navy, German 6, 21, 33, 47, 51, 52, 104, 114, 135, 136, 138
Nazi(s) 90–103, 106–108, 110, 111, 118, 122, 124, 131–133, 143, 145
Nazi–Soviet Pact 108, 110, 121
Neuilly, Treaty of 53
New Deals 63–67
Night of the Long Knives 95
no man's land 35–7
Normandy landings 138, 139
North African campaign 120, 129, 130
Norway/Norwegian 5, 6, 111, 113, 132, 133
nuclear missiles 151, 154–156
nuclear science, development in 15, 16, 145, 151
Nuclear Test-Ban Treaty 151, 156
Nuremberg 92, 93, 103
Nuremberg Laws 96

Okhrana 69, 71, 84
Okinawa, Battle of 144, 145
Omaha Beach 139

Operation Barbarossa 121
Operation Dynamo 113
Operation Eagle 114, 116, 117
Operation Overlord (D-Day) 138
Operation Pied Piper 109
Operation Sea Lion 114, 116, 117

Pacific, war in the 125–127, 134, 144–146
Pact of Steel 89
Pals battalions 25, 41
Pankhurst, Emmeline 18, 32
Paris 6, 9, 16, 17, 26, 27, 47, 53, 97, 113, 139
Park, Air Marshal 115
Passchendaele, Battles of 40, 43, 44, 46
Pearl Harbor 125, 127
'perestroika' 157
Pétain, Marshal 113
Petrograd 72–77, 80
Philippine Sea, Battle of 144
'Phoney' war 110
Pluto (oil pipelines) 138
Poland/Polish 15, 17, 51, 53, 55, 68, 77, 97, 108, 110, 111, 113, 116, 121, 124, 131, 141, 146, 148–150, 152, 157
Potsdam Conference 148–150
poverty (in USA) 61
Prague 'Spring' 150
propaganda 19, 20, 30, 31, 46, 82, 85, 88, 89, 93, 94, 135, 149
purges, Stalin's 83

Quantum Theory 15
Quebec 9

'race to the sea' 27
radar 115, 116, 136, 154
radio 9, 31, 57, 58, 84, 88, 93, 100, 102, 112, 118, 121
radium 15, 16
Rasputin 73
rationing 30, 32, 118
Reichstag 94
Relativity, Theory of 15
Remagen 142
reparations 51–53, 91, 148
Resistance activities 132, 133, 139, 143
Rhineland 51, 104, 106, 107
Röhm, Ernest 95
Romania 5, 28, 53, 61, 141, 148, 149, 152, 157
Rome–Berlin Axis 89
Rommel, General 112, 120, 129, 130, 138
Roosevelt, Franklin D 63–67, 125, 145, 147, 148
Russia/Russian 5, 6, 21–23, 26–29, 46, 48, 50, 51, 56, 60, 68–85, 105, 108, 110, 120–124, 128–130, 132, 137, 141, 142, 146–157
Russian Revolution (of 1905) 72
Russian Revolution (of 1917) 50, 60, 68, 74–76, 150
Rutherford, Ernest 15

SA 90–97
St Germain, Treaty of 53
St Petersburg 69, 71, 72, 84
St Valentine's Day Massacre 59
Saar 51, 105–107, 109
Sachsenhausen extermination camp 97
Salerno, landings at 130
SALT talks 151
Sarajevo, assassination at 22
Schlieffen Plan 26, 27
scientific advances 7–16
'scorched earth' policy 122
Serbia/Serbian 22, 23, 29
Sèvres, Treaty of 53
'show trials' 85
Singapore, loss of 126
Solidarity (Polish trade union) 150
Somme, Battle of the 31, 39–43, 46
Spitfire (air fighter) 115
sport 8, 10

Sputnik 151
SS 92, 94–97, 100, 110, 122, 131, 142, 143
Stalin, Josef 74, 76, 80–85, 105, 121, 122, 147–150, 152
Stalingrad 84, 128, 130, 137
START Treaty 151
Star Wars (SDI) 151
'Strength Through Joy' 101, 102
Streseman, Gustav 91, 92
submarines/U-boats 33, 42, 51, 127, 135, 136, 140, 151, 156
Sudetenland 107, 108
suffragettes 17, 18, 19, 20
suffragists 18, 19

tanks 31, 39, 40, 41, 47, 112, 113, 120, 123, 129, 130, 141, 152, 154
Tannenburg, Battle of 28
Teheran Conference 147
telephone, use of 9, 57
Tennessee Valley Authority (TVA) 64
'Tin Lizzies' (Model T Fords) 13, 41, 57
Titbits magazine 10
Tito, Marshal 132, 149
Tobruk, Battle over 120, 129
transport, new forms of 12
Treblinka extermination camp 124
trench warfare 27, 31, 34–37, 40, 88
Trianon, Treaty of 53
Triple Alliance 6, 21, 26
Triple Entente 6, 21, 26
Trotsky, Leon 75, 76, 78, 85
Truman, Harry S 145, 148, 149
Tsar Nicholas II 23, 46, 50, 69, 70, 72–75, 77, 78
Turkey/Turkish 21, 22, 28, 29, 47, 49, 51, 53, 55, 87, 105, 155, 156
tyre, pneumatic 12

Ultra (intelligence) 134, 135
United Nations 147, 148, 157
unemployment crisis, German 101
unemployment crisis, USA 63–67
Union of Fascists, British 86, 87
United States/America 7–9, 11, 13, 14, 28, 31, 33, 38, 42, 46, 47, 50, 54–68, 78, 92, 109, 114, 116, 119, 121, 122, 125–127, 129, 130, 136, 137, 139, 143–157
Unknown Warrior 48
uranium 15, 16

V1 and V2 missiles 140
V3 long-range gun 140
VE Day 142
Verdun, Battle over 40, 43
Versailles, Treaty of 50–53, 92, 104, 108, 148
Victor Emmanuel (King of Italy) 89
Victoria/Victorian 5, 7, 158
Vichy 113
Vimy Ridge, Battle of 40
Vittorio Veneto, Battle of 28
VJ Day 146

Wall Street Crash 62, 92
Warsaw 16, 110, 124, 141
Warsaw Pact 150, 152
wartime auxiliary service 118, 119
'WASP' 60
Western Front 27–29, 32, 34–47, 90
White Russians 77–79, 141
Wilson Woodrow 49, 50, 53, 54, 56
Winter Palace, storming of the 76
wireless telegraphy 9, 10, 138
women's role/issues 17, 18, 19, 20, 32, 49
Wright brothers 14

Yalta Conference 147–148
Young Pioneers 84
Ypres, Battles of 27, 38, 40, 43, 44, 47
Yugoslavia 53, 120, 132, 141, 149